My *Sweet* Encounter with DEATH

ANA CHRISTINA

WESTBOW
PRESS®
A DIVISION OF THOMAS NELSON
& ZONDERVAN

Scripture quotations taken from the Amplified® Bible, Classic Edition (AMPC), Copyright © 1954, 1958, 1962, 1964, 1965, 1987 by the Lockman Foundation. Used by permission. www.Lockman.org

Scripture quotations, as noted, are from the ESV® Bible (The Holy Bible, English Standard Version®), copyright © 2001 by Crossway, a publishing ministry of Good News Publishers. Used by permission. All rights reserved.

Scriptures taken from the Holy Bible, New International Version®, NIV.® Copyright ©1973, 1978, 1979, 2011 by Biblica, Inc. Used by permission of Zondervan. All rights reserved worldwide. www.zondervan.com. The "NIV" and "New International Version" are trademarks registered in the United States Patent and Trademark Office by Biblica, Inc.

WestBow Press books may be ordered through booksellers or by contacting:

WestBow Press
A Division of Thomas Nelson & Zondervan
1663 Liberty Drive
Bloomington, IN 47403
www.westbowpress.com
844-714-3454

ISBN: 978-1-4908-2016-3 (sc)
ISBN: 978-1-4908-2017-0 (hc)
ISBN: 978-1-4908-2015-6 (e)

Library of Congress Control Number: 2013922865

Print information available on the last page.

WestBow Press rev. date: 05/03/2023

Dedicated to

All the Souls who have been murdered by a loved one and their voices were never heard.

Contents

Acknowledgements

Reviewed by

Marie Oden is an author who is enthralled with the Word of God, and she takes great pleasure in the writing life. Whether it be fiction, non-fiction, or a compilation of women's devotional short stories, she ever seeks to be directed by God's Holy Spirit and inspire others to write what reflects our Redeemer's heart.

Fr. Gawargious A. Kolta, priest of St. John Coptic Orthodox Church in West Covina, California, since 1989. He earned a Bachelor of Science Degree in Chemistry in 1954, a Master of Science Degree in Physical Chemistry in 1958 and a Ph.D. in Physical Chemistry in 1962.

Fr. Abraam Ayoub, priest of St. Thomas Coptic Orthodox Church in Temecula, California, since 2007. He earned a Bachelor's in Medicine and Surgery in 2001. General Surgery Internship at Harbor UCLA 6/2005-6/2006. Internal Medicine residency in Loma Linda Medical Center 7/2006-11/2007.

Edited by

Joni Prinjinski lives in Old Town Keller, an old railroad town in Northern Texas. She provides editing and publishing services across the Internet for inspirational first-person stories, family entertainment, Messianic resources, and leadership training.

Copy edited, Stylistic edited, and Proof read by

Natoyah Alaka lives in Canada. She provides copy editing, stylistic editing, and proofreading services for materials such as: short stories, articles, documents and various letter writing.

Preface

I am no one. My life has been exceedingly private. Although moderately successful in my accounting career, I have no claim to personal fame. Despite my good childhood, I have grown up to suffer many of life's hardships, for which I was not prepared. I share this background with you because what will unfold in my story, and what distinguishes me now, is having gone through peril and discovering I was not alone, even when experiencing my own murder. Moment by moment, God was with me even in the unthinkable circumstances. I discovered that we do not have to wait until eternity to enjoy God's love and grace. I believe my true story will encourage many who are facing their own extreme hardships and failings to find comfort and strength.

I carefully weighed the intense difficulty of telling the details of my story against the need to share it with others. Among many other considerations, my own weaknesses and poor judgment are exposed in the telling of it, as well as intimate details of my life, and the lives of those involved. Wherever possible, I have disguised the names of persons involved, given those involved the benefit of the doubt, and eliminated any details not needed to communicate what I learned from all this. I could not eliminate all details, as the story requires disclosing some of them to be understood.

The following is a record of a spiritual journey. It was thrust upon me by circumstances I did not want or choose. It began with naivety on my part and continued with a mix of disappointments, struggles, and the beginning of insight. But dramatically my spiritual journey led me to a reality that, to me, cannot be contested. I was there, experienced it myself, and I'm a changed person. What was all-important to me before my encounter with death means little to me now; what was a nice, tame flicker of faith before is now vibrant and real.

I am no one, but I have been blessed. I believe my story could open a spiritual reality for you as well. My life has been exceedingly private, but I want to share my life-changing encounter with you. This is my testimony.

Coming of Age

I adjure you, O daughters of Jerusalem,
by the gazelles or the does of the field,
that you not stir up or awaken love
until it pleases.

—Song of Solomon 3:5 (ESV)

My Fairy-Tale Romance

Waiting in my study room on a sunny warm spring day, I heard the knock at the door. As I walked towards it, I wondered what the tutor would look like this time around; Short, chubby, old? I opened the door and there stood a six feet tall handsome man dressed in a sergeant uniform. He greeted me with his warm brown eyes and charming smile, as he introduced himself as Sam.

I loved each of our tutoring sessions, wishing he could stay longer. From that day on, I could not wait to hear his knock at the door. During each session, I knew I was falling in love with him. It did not matter to me that he was twenty-five and I was only fifteen.

Struggling with a Difficult Discovery

My story begins in Alexandria, Egypt. I was blessed with an exceptionally comfortable childhood. My parents had the resources to make sure my two sisters, my two brothers, and

I, were never in lack. We were Coptic Orthodox Christians, a religious minority in Egypt. The Coptic Orthodox Church is the predominant Christian religion in the country. It is one of the oldest branches of this faith, founded by the apostle Mark. A church still thriving despite centuries of persecutions and martyrdom.

Despite my parents' upper-class status, they were humble and kind-hearted. They often emphasized that our home was open to everyone. My mother was a simple, down-to-earth, loving, and generous lady. She loved and respected my father dearly. My father was a true gentleman who cherished my mother. He treated her with the deepest love, respect, and kindness. I grew up assuming that all men were made like him.

During my early childhood years, a significant change took place. My younger brother Steve was born with a cognitive disability. He needed special medical care, which was not available in Egypt. My parents knew that moving to Canada would enable them to provide him with the necessary care. I was seven years old when we migrated to Canada in the late 1960s. My father also wanted us to learn our native language and embrace our culture. Thus, a few years later, he decided to move us back to Egypt. This created a disconnect for me with the Arabic language, since I was now fluent in English. This led to me requiring a tutor by the age of 15.

While in Egypt, my parents enrolled my two sisters Mira and Nadia, and me, in a Catholic school for girls, where I attended grades five to nine. It was challenging to adapt back to the Egyptian culture. Our friends and schoolmates considered us "the liberal Canadians." I made many friends, yet I still felt that I did not quite belong. I continued to have difficulties with the Arabic language, nonetheless, I managed to get by and pass my courses. Grade nine was different, though. Students had to pass an intense government exam before entering into grade ten. For this reason, my father hired tutors to help me with geography and history, in Arabic.

When my father hired Sam, I was delighted. I could not help but fall head over heels for him! I was crushed when I later learned that Sam was a Muslim. Our faith and culture did not condone relationships between Orthodox Christians and Muslims. It was forbidden to marry another from the opposite faith. The religious walls of separation stood high within Egyptian society then, and still do today.

How could this mismatch have happened? When Bill, my brother-in-law, introduced Sam to our family, he lied about his faith. He told my father that Sam was a Christian, in hopes that he would give his buddy the tutoring job.

If I had known he was Muslim, I would have guarded my heart from falling in love with him. I would have known it would be impossible for us to pursue a relationship. However, it did not take long for Sam to declare his strong feelings towards me. We continued to see each other during the summer, until my father decided to send me back to Canada in the fall.

Despite the separation, our love remained resilient. We stayed in touch over the next few years by writing letters and by phone calls. When I visited Alexandria during the summer months, we would meet.

I was not allowed to have a boyfriend; therefore, during these dreamy summer days, we met secretly. Every time I wanted to see Sam, I snuck out of my parents' beach house. One of our favorite places to meet was on the beach behind the surfboard rental shack. The surfboards were stacked high, forming a barricade that made it difficult for anyone to see us. One time, however, a beach patrol officer scolded us when he spotted us sneaking around. I begged him not to report to my parents, knowing they would end my social life immediately. He agreed, after Sam slipped him a couple of Egyptian pounds.

Moving back to Canada, after living in Egypt for five years, was difficult. Even though I did not quite feel that I belonged in Egypt, now I felt I did not quite belong in Canada. It was difficult to make new friends in high school; it took a long time to feel a sense of belonging. Having Sam's letters and phone calls was what kept me going at times.

By the time I was twenty, our love had become much stronger. I decided to bring the news to my father and let him know that we wanted to get married. My father was furious when he learned about our relationship. He liked Sam but could not allow me to marry a non-Christian. I tried to explain to him that Sam was willing to travel to Canada. We could get married there and no one would know about our religious differences or even care.

As predicted, my father made it crystal clear that this would only happen over his dead body. When I saw how upset my father became, I finally realized that I had to forget Sam, once and for all. I could not dishonor my father. I loved and respected him too much to bring this shame upon our family by marrying outside our religion. My dad held a rather high position in Egypt and was well known and respected by many. Although it grieved me, the thought of having to end my relationship, I made the decision to do so. It pained Sam as well but he understood. From then on, I moved on with my life.

Daisy Petals

Years later, in the summer of 1984, I flew from Canada to the United States to visit my cousin and his wife. During my summer stay in California, I met Paul. He was a pleasant man who courted and pursued me; his eagerness was endearing. In the little time we spent together, he showered me with flowers and took me to the finest restaurants. He appeared to be a generous man.

After I returned to Canada, Paul and I would talk for hours on the phone, as our bond grew stronger. He sent me flowers every week and he gave me cards flowing with pages of hand-written poetry. He treated me like a princess. Even though I was not in love with him, I felt that I would eventually fall in love with him. Paul was rushing me to marry him. He was of the same Christian faith, plus Egyptian, so of course, my family approved of him. My answer was "yes" when he proposed, and we married in California, in October of that year.

It did not take long before Paul revealed his true character. The day after our honeymoon he went to work, I was home that day, so I unpacked all our wedding gifts and displayed them in his wall unit. I was excited for him to come home and see the embellishment of the living room. I had arranged the wall unit with all the fine china, crystals, and silverware.

When Paul arrived home, he looked at the wall unit, and did not say a word. For the rest of the evening, he continued with his silent treatment. Confounded, I asked him what was wrong and tried several times to get him to open up to me, but he refused to respond. I assumed something upsetting must have taken place at his work and that he was not able to speak to me about it.

After three weeks of total silence, Paul decided to finally have a conversation with me. This happened after I had written him a long letter demanding that we talk. His first words were, "How dare you move my knickknacks!" I was so shocked and confused. I could not believe that arranging the wall unit with our memorabilia, was what upset him to this extent. I thought he would have appreciated it, since it was for us.

I realized from this moment, our marriage was headed early into tribulations. These hostile interactions continued and manifested themselves in different ways. The man I had married was not the same generous man who had showered me with love, kindness, and consideration. He revealed himself as cold, critical, controlling, selfish, and materialistic.

I was married to a narcissist and did not know it at the time. The word *narcissist* did not exist in my vocabulary. During those days, the Internet and Google were not available. Therefore, there was no way to find information about other women whom suffered this similar fate. I did not know that narcissism was a character disorder and could not be changed. I continued on without truly understanding my situation. My husband's behaviour extended into every aspect of our relationship and beyond.

One thing I found odd about him, was that he had not contacted his family in Egypt for ten years. There was no conflict between them; Paul just did not want to be bothered by them. He had two brothers and two sisters; he was the youngest. He had lost both his parents when he was young and his oldest sister ended up raising him. She was devastated when he decided to leave Egypt and migrate to the United States. She was heartbroken over him but he did not care. I finally found his brother's phone number and called him in Egypt and put Paul on the phone. His family members were delighted to hear his voice after all these years. They had a great conversation and Paul maintained communication with all his siblings.

A few years later, my older sister Nadia came to visit us from Canada, along with her daughter and husband. Nadia quickly fell in love with beautiful California weather and wanted to move to the area. Within a week, she managed to land a position at a travel agency. She was ecstatic and told us the news over dinner, which made me beyond happy, as I longed for my sister to live close to me.

I had no other immediate family members living in California. The idea of having my sister nearby was comforting to me; however, Paul was opposed to it. The following morning, I overheard him talking to the hiring manager of the travel agency. Paul threatened to call immigration on him if he did not rescind the job offer to Nadia. She was a Canadian citizen and still required a work visa. The owner was already planning on obtaining a work permit for her, through NAFTA, now known as CUSMA. As a result of Paul's threats, he decided not to hire Nadia and withdrew the job offer.

Nadia and her family returned to Canada extremely disappointed. Especially after learning from the owner of the travel agency, what Paul had done.

A similar situation occurred when my brother Fred and his wife came to California. He had just graduated as a System Analyst from DeVry Institute in Arizona. There was a job employment agreement between US Immigration and the Institute. If Fred landed a job within six months of his graduation, he would be granted a permanent work visa. He was hoping to land a job quickly, and I offered him and his family to stay at our house in the meantime.

Fred and his wife occupied our guest room most of the time to remain out of Paul's way, but Paul still went out of his way to make them feel unwelcome and uncomfortable. He said to me, "As long as your brother is here, I will make your life a living nightmare," and he kept his word.

Fred applied for many jobs, but he never received a call for an interview. In those days, people depended on landlines and Fred had access to one of our telephones. The answering machine happened to be located in Paul's office, which was locked. We found it suspicious that Fred was not receiving any calls. After all, he had graduated top of his class and most of his colleagues had already obtained jobs. There was a high demand for their specialization during that time. Fred suspected Paul was erasing messages from the answering machine. I really hoped he would land a job in California, especially close to us.

A month passed and Paul decided that he did not want my brother staying with us any longer. He threatened that they needed to leave or else he was going to call the police to kick them out. I refused his demands, so he raised his voice to make sure they heard him. I pleaded with him to lower his voice, but he continued to yell louder. That same night my brother and his wife packed their car and left. They departed extremely hurt and disappointed and headed back to Canada.

Paul had succeeded in getting his way again with my family. I was disturbed and disgusted on how far he would go to make sure I had no family members around. He wanted to completely isolate me to have complete control. It is ironic how I went out of my way to connect him with his family, yet he went out of his way to isolate me from mine.

A narcissist is controlling and manipulative with an inflated sense of self-importance. Life evolves only around his or her needs. Narcissists are extremely selfish and lack empathy for others. They have a sense of entitlement and look down on people they feel are inferior to them. They feel best when they belittle another to make themselves feel superior. They become emotionally unavailable, the more a person shows them love. To mask their insecurities, they will break down a person's self-esteem to boost their own. They are critical of others and always believe that they are in the right. They are like vampires. In my case, I was depleted emotionally and financially.

Paul often argued over simple things, but most of the time it was over money, which made our lives miserable. Ironically,

I was making more money than him, but it did not matter. Sadly, I learned to give in to him most of the time just to avoid conflicts. When he did not get his way, he enjoyed resorting to giving me the silent treatment. This took a toll on me emotionally and physically. As a result, I was often drained and ill from the constant arguing and hostility in our home.

The only times Paul showed any compassion, were during intimacy or when I was sick. He would always take good care of me during these moments. It was strange, it was as if I were married to two different men, but when I look back now, it all makes sense—a narcissistic person must have control, and when I was in these vulnerable situations, he did not need to break me to gain control.

In 1989, Nadia was going through a deep depression. She lived in Canada and wanted to get away from her environment and come visit me. She called me asking if I could buy her a plane ticket—Nadia was having financial difficulties and could not afford to buy it.

I spoke to Paul about what my sister was going through and that I needed to book her a flight. He suggested that since she would not be able to reimburse us, she would need to give us one of her gold bracelets. This would cover the cost of the ticket, which was $350 US dollars. I did not like Paul's request, but unfortunately our bank accounts were shared. If I sent her the money without his consent, I knew he would make her feel uncomfortable during her stay. Making Nadia feel bad would defeat the whole purpose of her visit. I told my sister what Paul proposed—she agreed to give him what he requested upon her arrival. However, Paul insisted that she send us the bracelet first, before we would consider buying the plane ticket. When I informed Nadia of his request, she was offended and told me that she no longer wished to come.

Despite Paul's behavior, it was difficult to leave him. We were married and it was against our church to divorce, but I knew I had to get out. It did not make sense to stay in such a toxic relationship. The day I was packing to leave, I discovered I was pregnant and reluctantly shared the information with Paul. He begged me to stay and promised he would change his ways. Being accustomed to this routine, I told him that I did not believe in his empty promises. He pleaded that he was willing to cut his arm, with a knife, and with his blood, write on the wall how much he loved me. He emphasized that my sadness and stress would poison my bloodstream, and in turn, hurt the baby. He promised to ensure I would never be sad or upset again, at least for the sake of the baby.

I did not believe that Paul would never upset me again. However, I gave him the benefit of the doubt that his seven months of civility and peace would become a new habit.

On my fourth month of being pregnant with our son Andrew, my sister Nadia committed suicide. I never forgave myself for allowing Paul to control the situation, to the point that I failed to do the right thing by my sister. I regretted not insisting on her coming to visit me to get a break when she was going through her deep depression. I wanted to avoid my sister being in a hostile environment, as to why I didn't push for her to come and visit. At the same time, if I had sensed that my sister was suicidal, I would have insisted she come, regardless of the situation in my home.

As expected, Paul could not keep his promise of not upsetting me during my pregnancy. A narcissist cannot help but have a lack of empathy. I had a miserable pregnancy and continued to be unhappy throughout our marriage.

Four years later, we were having dinner with my cousin and his wife when we somehow got on the topic of divorce. I made a remark about the idea of hiring a divorce lawyer. Paul right away, in front of everyone, boasted, "I can also hire a sniper." My cousin looked at him and said, "Paul, what are you saying?" He responded, "Well, if she hires a lawyer, I will hire a sniper and I will easily get away with it, because the day she leaves me I will lose my mind and no judge would hold me accountable for my actions." We all sat in silence, digesting the threats that my husband had just made.

I knew I had to get out of this toxic marriage once and for all, but I found out I was pregnant again, this time with my daughter Colleen. I decided to stay despite his earlier threat to me. It seemed that God did not want me to leave. The children were the best thing that came out of that marriage. They were my blessings from above.

We were all negatively affected by Paul's behavior. His selfishness and constant arguing were tearing the family apart. As the years passed, I struggled to balance a high-stress job with an increasingly stressful marriage. The children were torn and devastated, as they saw the constant arguing and fighting. They were always caught in the middle.

I wanted the marriage to work, especially for the sake of the children. I also knew that God hated divorce, according to scripture. In efforts to improve and maintain our marriage, I sought counseling from our church. For thirteen years, priests and counselors gave us their guidance, but nothing changed.

One evening, I came home late after attending a concert with my mother and family friends. The following morning, Paul threatened that the next time I came home late, he would slit my throat. But he didn't end his threat there—he elaborated on how he would take my blood and write on the walls how horrible a mother I was. This is how he wished the children to remember me. I never understood what set him off in such an exaggerated manner.

In the late 90s, I was gifted a book on my birthday, called The Power of Positive Thinking, by Dr. Norman Vincent Peale. That book changed my life. In the first chapter, Dr. Peale asks the reader to repeat out loud the words, I can do all things through him who strengthens me (Philippians 4:13, ESV). He then asked the reader to repeat this sentence several times throughout the day. At first, I ignored his instruction, but later I found myself reciting the words. As I repeated it throughout the day, I started believing and feeling the power of the mantra.

As the days, weeks, and months passed, I became boldly empowered by that statement. I started a much closer walk with God—I started to feel stronger. Paul's words of criticism and destruction had less affect on my emotions and health less and less every day.

I had concluded that it would be impossible to handle a divorce from a difficult man like Paul, and maintain my professional performance at work. Over the years, I had met co-workers who were going through divorces. The stress of a divorce took an emotional toll on them and negatively affected their work. Later that year, I left my job and became determined to take advantage of the time to get out of my toxic marriage, with as little conflict and personal suffering as possible.

I hired a reputable lawyer who managed to get a restraining order against Paul. He was immediately removed from our home. Finally, the house was peaceful without his hostility swirling around us. The kids were relieved as well. We were living in harmony—no fighting no arguing. We finally had peace.

Our Coptic Orthodox Church and community frowned upon divorces. There were few divorces in the Coptic Christian community back in the 90s. At first, I felt I did not need a divorce, that a permanent separation would be healthy for the children and myself. But as I was getting control over my finances, I discovered that Paul had opened several credit cards in my name, without my consent. He wracked them all up, totalling over $60,000 and forged my signature on all the applications. To put a stop to him using my credit, and to separate his liabilities from mine, I had no choice but to purse a divorce. A legal separation was not going to be enough to regain control over my finances.

I finally accepted that it was better for my children to grow up in a single parent home with peace and harmony, than to live with both parents in such a toxic environment. I observed that children whom were raised by both parents, in such situations, resorted to drugs to escape their reality.

I had believed a divorce would end all the conflict. That I would be able to surround my children with love, care, and a sense of well-being, but, again, I was so naïve. The conflict arising from the divorce, and the custody battle that followed, took a drastic toll on Andrew and Colleen. It became worse than the thirteen years of marriage. Now I understood why our Lord hates divorce. He never forbade it, but He states He hates it because of the consequences and negative affects it has on children.

Marriage is a complicated relationship at best. I discovered that a piece of paper from a court, does not solve all the issues within a family. For one, Paul was still the father of our two children. He had a say in their lives, just as much as I did. I eventually learned that if I wanted peace within our family, I still had to accommodate Paul. More hard lessons would lie ahead for all of us.

Fresh Start

Above all else, guard your heart,
for everything you do flows from it.
—Proverbs 4:23 (NIV)

First Love Returns

It was a beautiful sunny New Year's Day. I had just come home from the movies with the children when the phone rang. The voice on the other end was sweet and familiar. It was Sam. Yes, my first love, Sam. He was vacationing in Florida and dissected California on the internet, searching for my phone number. He had been trying to find me for several weeks.

At first, we were so excited to reconnect that we spoke every day on the phone. I liked hearing his voice, but knew that I could not be with him again. I had just become a newborn Christian and did not want to disappoint my Lord by falling in love with a non-Christian at this stage of my life. Therefore, Sam decided to go back to Egypt a few weeks later.

In April, I planned a trip to Egypt to visit my mother, who had moved back to Egypt from Canada after my sister Nadia had died. My mother was on her own since my father had died in a horrible car accident, in 1982. At the time, my mother was staying with my two brothers, Steve and Fred.

Once Sam found out I was in Egypt, he invited me out for lunch. I accepted his invitation, as I convinced myself that my heart was guarded, and thought it would be nice to see him after all these years, for old times' sake.

My heart started beating fast as Sam walked up to my table. I was shocked by how the walls around my strongly-guarded heart started to crumble, as he touched my hands to greet me with a warm smile and an intense hug. It was as if we never separated for those almost twenty-five years. I discovered that he had the character of my ideal man. He was kind and gentle, a good listener, as well as tender and romantic. He swept me off my feet and I fell deeply in love with him all over again.

I felt that we were each other's destiny. I was so touched when I found out that Sam still had all four of the cassette tapes we had exchanged twenty-five years ago. These tapes had all our love songs on them. At the time, we had bought two sets of each tape; each of us had written "I love you" on the cassette cases in: English, French, Italian, and Arabic.

We had something else in common—loveless marriages. He was as unhappy in his marriage as I had been in mine. Both of us were looking for love. We wanted many of the same things.

I went back to the States and Sam followed me a few months later, after he finalized his divorce with his wife. He treated my children with so much love and kindness. Andrew and Colleen loved Sam; they referred to him as Uncle Hany. They were both longing for a kind father figure. Paul, their father, had not been faithful in practicing his court visitation rights to see the children, which was devastating for them.

I remember on Andrew's eighth birthday, he sat at the curb side waiting for his father to pick him up for dinner. Andrew refused to go inside the house despite waiting for several hours without his father showing up or calling him. He kept saying, "Daddy will show up as he promised. He will be here." Sadly, his dad never showed up nor did he call him, so Andrew finally gave up and went inside the house with a broken heart.

The children were overjoyed when Sam and I announced that we were getting married. I knew I would disappoint my family and friends by marrying a non-Christian, but I could not resist Sam this time. I believed it was destiny that we reconnected. During this time, I felt so vulnerable and deprived. I had longed for the love and kindness of a good man that I was not able to walk away.

One morning, I received a call from one of the Coptic Orthodox priests, whom I loved and respected. It had been over seven years, since I heard from him. He sounded disturbed on the other end of the phone and asked me if I was all right. I answered quickly that I was doing great and asked him why he was calling. He said he just had a dream where I was lost and he was out in the streets looking for me and could not find me. He suddenly woke up and felt he had to call me and check on me. When I look back now, I know that this was a warning from the Lord, but having already made up my mind and confident in my decision, I did not consider I was making the worst decision of my life.

Sam agreed that we would get married in a church, and that was a big step for him. He even met with one of our Coptic Orthodox bishops, who talked to him about Jesus and Christianity. Sam was taken by him, but he did not convert. He believed that Jesus could have been the Son of God, but Sam got hung up on

ana Christina

the Trinity. He was struggling with accepting that God, Jesus, and the Holy Spirit were one. This was a hurdle he would have to get over before being baptized in our church.

Nonetheless, Sam and I were still planning on getting married in the Coptic Church and we were working on that goal. I had applied for a divorce in our church and was granted the divorce and permission to remarry, but Paul appealed the church's decision. In the meantime, he also found out that Sam was Muslim, which of course made him furious. I had to rethink our decision to marry in the Coptic Church. Doing so, would indicate that Sam was baptized in a Church. This event is all Paul would have needed to report to any Muslim organization. It is against their law for any Muslim to convert and be baptized. The penalty would be death for him, his two children, and me—my children would not be affected by this law.

Since I knew that Paul would go to any length to get rid of me in order to gain custody of the children, Sam and I were married later that year in a nondenominational church. The Coptic Church does not recognize any marriage outside its church. Thus, my marriage was considered an act of unfaithfulness. This resulted in Paul winning his appeal for permission for him to remarry in the Coptic Church.

When the children knew that Sam and I were going on a honeymoon, they cried and begged to go with us. They didn't want to stay with their father. The only way I could get them to accept going to their father's house was to let them know that I would send the nanny with them, to stay during the time we were gone. Paul had agreed to having the nanny with the children for that week, but I found out later that he had let her go on the first day.

Two days into the honeymoon, I received a call from the principal of Andrew's school. She told me that Andrew was crying all morning, and had asked to speak to me.

"Mommy, daddy said that the devil is living inside of you now."

"What? No dear, why would daddy say that?"

"Daddy said that you and uncle Hany are living in sin and you did not really get married."

"But we did get married, you were there at the wedding with all our friends and family."

"Yes mommy, but he said because it was not in an Orthodox church, it was not a real wedding and now God is upset at you, and left you, and the devil is living inside of you instead."

"No dear, that is not true, it was a real church and a real wedding and God is not upset at me, and definitely there is no devil living inside of me."

"Are you sure mommy?"

"Yes, I am sure dear, daddy is talking nonsense. When I come back home, I will take you and Colleen and we will go to church together."

"Ok mommy, I miss you and can't wait to see you."

"I miss you too dear and I will be back home in five days, I love you so much, Andrew."

My heart was broken over Andrew's sadness and confusion. I realized that Paul was starting a new tactic to turn the children against me.

Initially, Sam and I lived with the children quietly with so much love and understanding. As a Certified Public Accountant (CPA), I became the sole provider. I always had executive positions as a Director or Chief Financial Officer of a company. When it came to jobs, Sam was not able to find anything substantial because of his imperfect English and lack of work experience in the US. He decided to stay home and care for the children and the household.

I enjoyed working, so I did not mind being the breadwinner. I loved Sam so much that I didn't even mind also supporting his two daughters and ex-wife whom were living in Egypt. He was a great cook and had a hot meal ready for me at the end of each day. I much appreciated this because I did not have the energy to do it after a long day at work.

The peace I enjoyed with Sam at home rejuvenated my energy every evening. I would start my day fresh the following morning, ready to embark on another long, hard day at the office.

We enjoyed our lifestyle, routine, and each other's company. We felt we were soul mates and we did not make any friends, as we did not need anyone else. The children enjoyed the peace and harmony between us, as it reflected positively on them. We never quarreled or disagreed. Sam loved playing with the children and always took them swimming and bike riding. Our marriage was like a fairy-tale love story. I never thought two people at our age could find each other, after all these years, and be this much in love and live happily with so much harmony.

Heartbreak and Hard Lessons

For the Lord, the God of Israel, says: I hate divorce
and marital separation and him who covers his
garment [his wife] with violence. Therefore, keep
a watch upon your spirit [that it may be controlled
by My Spirit], that you deal not treacherously
and faithlessly [with your marriage mate].
—Malachi 2:16 (AMPC)

Seeking Peace for My Kids

Problems began to surface. Paul was angry that our children were being raised in a home with a different man. He tried many ways to make a case for gaining custody of Andrew and Colleen. Sam and I were constantly back and forth in court and at police stations, defending ourselves against false accusations. One of the claims accused Sam of being a Muslim terrorist who owned a gun, which he supposedly pointed at Andrew's head. We were also accused of smoking drugs and giving them to the children. On one occasion, Andrew was taken to the emergency room by his father. He filed a false claim that Sam beat him up, threw him down the stairs, and broke the phone over his head. Every time Paul filed a false claim, Sam and I had to go in front of a judge and prove our innocence. Every time the judge would award my children back to us. I had to use police assistance to pick up the kids from Paul's house at the end of every visitation time, because he refused to just drop them back to me.

It was inevitable that his distain for me would rub off on the children. Paul managed to brainwash them against Sam and instructed them to defy us. Paul was hoping that the children would push Sam's buttons to the point that he may retaliate against them and hurt them. This was the only way Paul could succeed in taking the kids away from me. I thank God that as much as these children became wild and unruly, Sam never lost his temper with them. But I was sad to see my children tormented and manipulated by Paul, month after month.

I will never forget Colleen's heart-piercing words to me when I was changing a light bulb in the ceiling. I was standing on a chair, and I asked her to hold the chair tight to prevent me from falling. She responded saying, "But Mom, if you fall you may die and all our troubles will go away."

I was shocked to hear what my six-year-old was saying to me. I got off the chair and held her in my arms and asked her as my tears streamed down my face, "Do you want Mommy to die, Colleen?"

"No, I don't, Mommy, but Daddy said if you die or go to Egypt and never come back, all our problems would go away." Now, tears streamed down her face. Her words broke my heart. The kids were in so much emotional pain. Paul had convinced them that the only way their pain would stop was if their mother disappeared from their lives.

After two years of this horrible custody battle and agony, I finally felt that this could no longer continue. I had to put an end to this madness and pain for my children. I knew that Paul would not stop fighting until he got his way and destroyed all of us. I was terrified we would end up losing the children to a foster home. Thus, I felt compelled to make a sacrifice to save my children. I was willing to give up my rights to the children to restore peace and order back into their lives. It was no longer about my right to have them; rather, it was about their right to have a peaceful and happy childhood. I made the difficult decision to give Paul sole custody of the children, which is what he was fighting for. Paul and I came up with an amicable agreement that he would keep the children during the week, and I would have them on weekends.

This custody agreement was confirmed in court. I gave up years of child support and alimony payments he owed me, amounting to over $80,000. I had found my place of peace and refuge, and I wanted my children to find peace as well. I just wanted us all to move on with our lives and have Paul concentrate on the well-being of the children. Instead of destroying them in the process of trying to hurt me.

Disappointments

A piece of paper called a marriage license cannot hold a marriage together. A slip of paper called a divorce decree, will not magically create decorum. Neither can a piece of paper called a custody agreement bring harmony. It takes well-adjusted adults to do that, and no law can transform the unwilling.

My first big disappointment was when Paul stopped allowing the children to stay overnight on the weekends. He convinced them that as long as Sam was there, they could not spend the night. This resulted in the children visiting for only a few hours on either Saturday or Sunday. He would never allow them to stay for a whole weekend; it was one day or the other. Paul would make sure to fill up their schedules. He soon convinced them that they could not visit me at all, as long as Sam was in the house. This new rule resulted in me having to ask Sam to leave the apartment for several hours until I finished my visit with my children. I could not always ask Sam to leave, so I sometimes had to visit with the children at a restaurant or at a movie theatre.

How I longed to have my children where we could be together in the privacy of our home! Then I could relax, watching them play, as I prepared their favorite meal, knowing how much they longed for it. All I wanted to do was hold them as we sat on the couch watching their favorite show. At bedtime, I would tuck them into their beds and make them breakfast in the morning. Simple things that every mother should be able to do with her children were no longer within reach. Sitting at a restaurant or at the movies was not the normal way to spend time with the children. I wanted more, but even this less-than-ideal arrangement deteriorated.

After counting the hours and waiting a whole week to see the kids, Paul would make it a habit to send me home empty-handed on the weekends. He did not care that we made plans; he had to control everything, and he was getting a kick out of it.

When I would go to pick up Colleen and Andrew from his place, I would often end up waiting a few hours in my car, in the parking lot of his apartment complex. At times, after having waited several hours, the children would come out crying, "Daddy changed his mind and is grounding us, so we can't go with you. You have to leave now."

Paul's interference in my relationship with my children was excessive. Sometimes Paul would assign Colleen random chores that she would have to do in order for her to be allowed to leave the house and have lunch with me. I constantly had to wait in the car until she was done with everything. She started waking up as early as 5:00 a.m. on a Saturday morning to finish all her work, which included cleaning the bathrooms. At one time, she finished ahead of schedule, got excited, and called me to come a little earlier. In that moment, Paul decided to have her wash all the shelves in the refrigerator. She was too little to carry those glass shelves. Terrified that she might break them, she would take extra time to clean everything. Meanwhile, I had to wait patiently in the car, again, until she was done.

This new arrangement was breaking my heart, but I did not want to drag the children back into court. The court system did not respect the outcome and the well-being for the kids—it was outrageous. This was bitterly disappointing to me. I wondered if justice, honesty, and mercy even existed anymore. Before we had reached our settlement agreement, Paul's lawyer did nothing but show up in court with my lawyer and always had a reason to ask for continuance. I spent over $70,000 on lawyers and never had a day in court.

Paul often taunted me, saying, "I would rather pay lawyers than give you a penny." He spoke as if the money involved was all his doing. All our assets were a joint effort. We owned three gas stations and two beautiful homes. It would have made sense for him to keep a house and for me to keep the other, but he wanted to fight until the end, forcing on us to lose everything. He had taken a second mortgage on our main house, which made the monthly payments unaffordable. I had a court order against him stipulating that he had to pay the mortgage. But he refused to pay, and I was forced to do a short sale on the house to save my credit. I received a settlement of a mere $12 on a house worth over a million dollars.

Later that year, I received an offer to be a Director of Finance at a lavish hotel in Dubai. Sam convinced me that he could only help me financially if we moved to the Middle East. He assured me he could easily find a white-collar job in an Arabic-speaking country. He used to work at a bank in Kuwait and felt that his experience would land him a good management job in any bank. Dubai was a growing tourist and commercial center, and I was convinced this move could work. By this time, I was financially depleted. One salary was no longer going to stretch far enough. We were still supporting Sam's ex-wife, as well as his two daughters. The girls were both attending medical school.

The new position offered me four weeks of paid vacation, plus four round-trip tickets to the US, each year. I felt that this new lifestyle could allow my kids to visit me during the summers in Dubai. This way, I would have quality time with them, far away from Paul's toxic interference and control. It would also allow me to visit them in the United States without Sam, which would offer my children and me more quality time. This arrangement would definitely be better than spending a few hours, every weekend, at a restaurant, park, or movie theater.

When I received the written offer, I went to court to obtain an order to have the children visit me. Strategically, Paul convinced the judge that because my husband was a Muslim, he feared that we might kidnap the children, take them to the Middle East, and then convert them to Islam, preventing them from returning to the States. It was a couple of years after the 9/11 tragedy. Everyone appeared to be apprehensive towards the Middle East and assumed all Muslims were terrorists. As a result of this bias, I was denied the right to have the children visit me in Dubai. However, I was allowed to visit them anytime in the US. The court order also stipulated that once I moved back to the United States, we would resume the previous court order where the children would spend every weekend with me.

My heart was torn. This was not the plan. I wanted the children to come and spend the summer with me in Dubai. Visiting them in the States was not going to be enough. I wanted to cancel my deal in Dubai, but I felt that the Lord wanted me to go. I did not understand why God would want me to leave, but other things were happening that showed me that He wanted me to go.

One early morning, I woke up anxious about my departure. Anxious about all the "unknowns" that lie ahead and wanted to cancel the whole thing. As I went for my early morning walk, I listened to a sermon on my headset. It was a sermon by Greg Laurie, and he was preaching about putting an "unknown" future in the hands of a "known" God. I felt that God was saying to me that it was going to be ok and to just trust that He would take care of things. Again, I felt He wanted me to go.

Another hint from God, was the last item on my "to do" list. I was to get a Christian CD from Calvary Church which had all the worship songs I loved. This way I would stay connected to the Word of God. I knew I would not be able to buy a Christian CD in the Middle East, nor would I be able to listen to Christian songs on the radio. The night before our departure, Sam and I went to the Calvary Church. To my disappointment, there were none available and the Church had not been able to get any in stock. I walked away discouraged and disappointed. We grabbed some coffee from the hallway and went inside the church to listen to what would be the last sermon before we left.

Once we finished our coffee, I decided to get up, before the sermon was over, and go throw away the empty cups in the trash can outside. As I was walking towards it, I noticed a CD lying on top of the can. I was in shock as I approached and realized that it was the exact CD I had wanted to buy. I trembled as I grabbed the discarded CD and walked back to the service sobbing. I was amazed that a big God could be thinking of my need and be so gracious and kind to gift me what I felt I needed that night. I was immersed in awe of God and filled with peace. He was sending me on my way. I felt His strong hands over this new journey and felt encouraged. He would deal with my heart issues and make a way to stay connected to my children through it all.

Dubai

Dubai was a beautiful city. The company provided us with a fully paid furnished four-bedroom flat, overlooking the bay. We enjoyed many of the company's perks, yet I went to bed many nights with tears running down my face. My heart ached—I longed for Andrew and Colleen. Moving away from the children was one of the hardest things I ever did.

The Hotel was undergoing a multi-million-dollar renovation and I soon realized that the general manager was corrupt. He was taking advantage of the owner who was the Minister of Education, a highly respected Sheikh, and a member of the Royal family. Three weeks had passed, since my arrival in Dubai and I received a phone call from a private number. The man on the phone stated that he was calling me on behalf of the Sheikh and instructed me to go to the front of the hotel. I was being summoned to the Sheikh's palace for a private meeting. He added that I would be picked up in fifteen minutes by a black car, which would take me to meet the Sheikh. I was not to tell anyone about this phone call, nor share where I was headed.

After the phone call, I immediately went to the main floor and waited at the front of the hotel. A black Rolls Royce pulled up with black tinted windows; I climbed inside. I was the only person in the back of the vehicle, while the driver drove in silence to the Palace. Upon arrival, I was escorted to the Sheikh's office. The Sheikh stood from behind his desk, greeted me, and offered me to have a seat. He wanted to know my assessment of the hotel's operations. I was candid and told him about the discrepancies and fraudulent transactions, I had observed. He ended the meeting by instructing that I go to my office at midnight, to receive further instructions through a fax. At exactly midnight, I received a fax which was addressed to all management from the Sheikh. It stated the following: "Effective immediately, Mr. Ferally is no longer the general manager of the hotel. Mrs. Ana Christina has been appointed interim general manager and will be overseeing the entire operations of the hotel."

The former general manager had fired most of the honest employees, especially the ones in the accounting department. He replaced them with corrupt agents whom were only loyal to him. I ended up restoring and bringing back all the honest employees and letting the dishonest ones go. In the United Arab Emirates, most blue-collar employees are not treated fairly and hardly have any rights. I was an advocate for those who were mistreated or abused. The employees were so happy to see justice done on their behalf and called me "an angel from Heaven." They felt I was the answer to their prayers. I also received the nickname "The Iron Lady." I was loved and respected by most of the employees at the hotel.

Sam was not able to land a job at a bank. He did not have enough recent job experience. Ironically, speaking and reading English fluently was mandatory in Dubai and throughout the Emirates. When Sam realized that he was not able to land a job on his own, he started hustling and bustling with all my influential friends to get help to open a business. He was especially focused on my lady friends whom were single or unhappily married. I saw a side of Sam that I had never seen before and I did not like it. He was a womanizer and a hustler. New tensions arose between us.

The Tide Turns Back to the USA

After trying this solution in Dubai for about two years, I could no longer continue living away from my children. My heart suffered extreme pain, especially after our short vacations together. Colleen wrote me a note for Valentine's Day the last time I saw her in the States which said: *Dear Mom, I love you so much... you are the best...I hope you never die...if you die my heart will die...if you leave me my heart will leave me...Happy Valentine's Day!* It was devastating to say goodbye to the kids and then return to Dubai. Another note said: *I wish I could live with you, your dotor* (daughter) *Colleen.* Being away from Andrew and Colleen tormented me more and more. I decided that I must move back to the US to tend to my children.

It became apparent that Sam did not have enough skills to find a decent job in Dubai. It did not make sense to stay there, since the whole purpose of moving to the Middle East was to improve our financial situation. Therefore, moving back to the US was the only option, but I was shocked to discover that I could not just leave the United Arab Emirates. I had taken out a loan for 220,000 Dirhams ($60,000 US) when we first moved to Dubai. We did not need to borrow that money, but Sam convinced me that it was a good idea to have it, in case we faced an emergency. I was not aware that the laws in the Emirates prevented one from leaving the country if he or she had a bank loan pending. A person is able to travel as long as he or she has a job waiting for their return. But once the person quits or is let go from the job, the company must call the banks and let them know the person no longer works for them. The bank will also submit the person's name to the airport, to prevent he or she from leaving the country until the debt has been paid.

My plan was to return the loan to the bank, since we did not need it, but I discovered that Sam had sent 100,000 Dirhams to his daughters and ex-wife in Egypt without telling me. I could not believe he did this behind my back. I trusted this man for years with all my money and hard work—I felt betrayed. As far as I was concerned, I could not trust him anymore. On top of that, Sam refused to move back to the US with me. Instead, he was insisting that I should take out another loan for him, so he could start a business in Dubai. I could not understand how he could make such ridiculous requests after all that he did. He knew taking another loan would bind me to staying in Dubai for several years longer. He knew I needed to return to the US to be with my children, and he knew hustling my women friends was inappropriate behaviour, yet he was not concerned. All of this destroyed my trust in him; I finally decided to end our marriage.

We divorced in Dubai a few months later. Now I understood why God wanted me to move to this city, temporarily. He needed me to see a side of Sam that I was not able to see while we were living in the US. These truths were only revealed under these new living conditions in Dubai. God wanted me to see Sam's true colors.

I had an interesting dream, which I did not understand at the time, but when I look back now, it was a warning from God. I dreamt that I was in my bedroom, afraid, sitting on my bed, as snakes were crawling everywhere on my bed and on the floor. My sister Nadia and my brother Fred appeared. They grabbed the snakes with their hands, throwing them outside the bedroom door, as fast as they could. They tried shutting the door, as more snakes were trying crawl back in. I woke up sweating and trembling.

At this point, all I wanted to do was go back to the US and be a mother again. I did not care about the powerful executive position I had or all the other perks. I just wanted to be with my children, but I did not have the money to pay off the loan. I talked to my employer about my situation. I offered to take an advance from them to pay off the loan and for me to make payments back to them from the US. I was amazed when they agreed to pay off my bank loan completely without me having to pay them back. They also gave me a great severance package. I felt very blessed and could clearly see God's hand leading me out of Dubai to be back with my children.

Colleen and Andrew were thrilled to hear about my divorce from Sam and my return to the US. They promised to be waiting for me at the airport. I was so eager to see my children. On the long flight home, I counted down the hours until I could see them and hug them. My spirit was grieved when they were nowhere to be seen at the airport. Their father refused to bring them to greet me. I should have learned by then to expect this from him.

My Humble Return

A joyful heart is good medicine,
but a crushed spirit dries up the bones.
—Proverbs 17:22 (ESV)

After returning to the US, I stayed at a friend's home for two months until I landed a job. I moved into an extended-stay hotel near my work. We had sold all our belongings before moving to Dubai, so all I had were two suitcases full of clothes.

I thought coming back without Sam would make the kids eager to come and stay with me, at least on the weekends. The court-ordered agreement stated that once I returned to the US, the custody would change from visitation to shared.

I dreamed of my children being able to sleep over. Unfortunately, that dream was not fulfilled. Paul prevented them from visiting me in the hotel and kept them overly busy on the weekends. I couldn't even pick them up to go to a restaurant or to a movie theatre.

I kept counting the hours until each weekend arrived in the hope that I would see Andrew and Colleen, but there was always an excuse from their father why I couldn't.

One day, I decided to go to their church on a Sunday morning hoping to see them. Unfortunately, Andrew was not there, but I was delighted to see Colleen, standing next to her stepmom. She was happy when she noticed me in the back of the church, but she was not allowed to come and stand next to me. She kept looking at me from the corners of her eyes, afraid to turn her head, in fear her father would scold her. He was standing in the back of the church watching in her direction. My heart ached as I longed to walk up to her and embrace her, but I knew that would make her uncomfortable. She was terrified of her father's reaction. After the service, I stayed around hoping she could sneak away and come and give me a hug. But she was rushed out of the building and I saw them drive away. My heart left with her.

As the weeks passed without seeing the children, I became lonely and depressed. After having all the power, clout, respect, and love from all my employees in Dubai, it became difficult to adjust to my new lifestyle of living alone in a hotel. I was starting to think that no one cared if I was dead or alive. I gave up that lavish lifestyle to be a mother again and enjoy my children, but the fulfillment of that dream was not within reach.

Not being able to see Colleen and Andrew was more than devastating. My spirit was crushed and I sank into a depression. I convinced myself that I was a failure on all fronts: A failure as a mother because my children did not want to be with me, a failure as a wife because I was divorced twice, a failure as a professional because I was too sick to concentrate and focus on my job. The more I concentrated on my disappointments, the more I fell into a deeper hole and lost complete hope. I could not forgive myself for all the mistakes I had made—I hated myself. The pain was too much to bear and I just wanted to die to gain peace. The depression was so deep, I began to consider how I might end it.

I started to pray every night that I would die in my sleep. I longed for death but could not take my own life. I was afraid I would go to Hell. Growing up in the Church, it taught that if one committed suicide, one would go straight to Hell. The Church considered it an act of murder. I wanted to leave this life of sadness and hopelessness, but committing suicide was not an option. God would have to take my life.

Every night, I prayed really hard that He would end my life. I became more depressed the following morning when I would wake up and discover I was still alive. Even at work, I would close the door and sit quietly holding my breath for a long time, hoping I would have a heart attack and just die—as if I could fool God by indirectly causing my own death.

It was obvious to me that I could no longer function at work. I had a highly visible job and needed to be mentally and emotionally sharp, so I decided to take a medical leave of absence from my work. I did not want to see anyone or be seen by others except by my children, but their father prevented even that. I did not have the energy or money to take Paul back to court and reinforce my court order. Instead, I stayed in my hotel room with the blinds closed, slipping into an ever deeper depression. I kept praying harder and harder that I would die because I wanted the torment and pain to end.

I had never understood how relentless and severe depression could be. There was no pill to take the pain away, nor could I pray it away— it was just torment. The act of simple thinking was tumultuous and caused me extreme anxiety. In my bitter grief, I found I could not smile back at anyone who initiated a smile. My heart was heavy with guilt, and my world became dark with no hope in sight. I thought about Nadia and felt her pain and what she must have endured with her suffering before she took her life.

Out of the Blue

Out of nowhere, Sam started calling me on my cell phone from Egypt. After speaking with me, he became alarmed about my depression. At first, I did not want to talk to him, yet I answered all his calls. He called like he was my lifeline and decided to fly back to the US to take care of me.

Sam took me to a psychiatrist who gave me several antidepressant medications. It took a while to identify the right medication that worked for me. Treating deep depression is tricky and everyone reacts differently to each medication. There was no magic pill to stop the mental and emotional pain. It was a long process to get out of and I could not do it alone. I needed someone to literally take me by the hand and get me the help I needed— and Sam did just that.

This depression was real and one of the most debilitating times in my life. I could not even think of the smallest of tasks. I felt helpless and hopeless. Sam took good care of me during my treatment; he made sure I ate well and gave me my medicine on time. Slowly, I got better and regained a little hope in life again, but I was still dependent on him. As the days passed by, he convinced me that we were meant for each other and that we should never separate again. He apologized for his terrible behavior in Dubai, and promised to never betray me again. He appeared sincere. I was still not back to my old self, and my spirit was still sad over everything that had happened.

About one month after his arrival, Sam began pushing for us to remarry. I did not want to marry Sam again, but he would not take no for an answer. I reluctantly remarried him in February of that year, while I was still not quite over my depression.

I wonder how many people continue to overlook the toxicities in their relationships and then choose to only focus on the good memories? While ignoring one's intuition and doubting obvious warnings signs.

After we moved into our new place together, Sam was back to his sweet and kind nature. He went over and above and treated me well. I eventually recovered and was able to return to the workforce. I landed a Director of Finance position and resumed the role of sole provider in our marriage.

Gradually, the children started to visit me for a few hours every other weekend, depending on their father's schedule. Although this did not comply with my court-awarded rights, I just accepted how things were and tried to make the best of it. It seemed at last there was some peace for us as a family and I was glad for that.

One important truth I learned from my struggles is that things do not always go the way we wish. Even when we do have a say, or have a court order, or want to fight for what is right, it is spiritually and financially exhausting.

A Mother's Heart

A couple of years passed and Colleen, now fourteen years old, wanted to come and live with me. Her father convinced her that he would give her up and allow her to live with me, provided I divorced Sam. I was frustrated because I could see that Paul was using Colleen to control my life and break my marriage. He managed to brainwash her to believe that the only option for her to live with me, was that I had to be divorced from Sam. Colleen was also adamant about us not going back to court and fighting over her—she hated court. I couldn't blame her. It was tormenting for her to watch her parents fight over her and Andrew. She witnessed how far her father would go to gain control and win. Now I had a new dilemma—I became anxious. Do I stay in my comfortable marriage or do I sacrifice it to finally have my daughter live with me again, after all these years of separation?

I started leaning towards sacrificing my life with Sam to provide Colleen a more stable life with me. I decided to speak to Sam and told him the dilemma I was facing and how it was tormenting me to stay with him knowing that my daughter needed me. Sam was furious! How could I contemplate leaving him? He felt that I was betraying him and choosing my children over him. He said, "Now that you are healthy and successful again you don't need me anymore." I could understand how frustrated he felt, but I remained conflicted about what to do.

Colleen was unhappy living with her dad. As she grew, he resented how she started to physically resemble me and how her voice started to sound similar to mine. People often pointed out how much she reminds them of me. Our features are very similar, but most of all our laugh is identical, so much that she was not allowed to laugh in her father's house.

As time passed, her father would call her derogatory names and criticize her because of her weight. One day, she called me crying from the Costco parking lot. She had spent a couple hours looking for her father who had abandoned her at the store. She could not get a hold of him by phone because he refused to answer. Colleen was searching for him all over the store and parking lot, walking in heels, after a Sunday church service. The poor thing was in pain from her little chubby legs rubbing against each other, and suffering in the exhausting midday heat. She finally found him at the end of the parking lot at the Costco gas station, sitting in his car. He wanted to teach her a lesson to never walk away from him again. His emotional abuse increased. Colleen finally opened up and told me how miserable she was living with her dad. I immediately hired a no-nonsense lawyer who filed an overnight action called "ex-parte." We took Paul to court the next day, and I was awarded full custody of Colleen, one of the best days of my life!

Colleen came to live with Sam and me; she was happy. Sam treated her well and she enjoyed being with us.

Andrew wanted to join his sister, but he still had issues with Sam's presence and was not comfortable with the idea.

He was also depressed living with his father. One evening after dinner at a restaurant, Andrew and I came back to my house to watch a movie. As I was getting out of the car, he took my keys and sat in the driver's seat; he wanted to drive away. I could see tears flowing down his cheeks. I asked him what was wrong and where he planned on going. He responded that he wanted to keep on driving until he drove off a cliff. He was so miserable living with his dad, yet felt he couldn't live at my house. I begged him not to drive away, but he would not listen, as he cried and told me he wanted to be left alone.

I was terrified for him in his desperation, but then a miraculous thing happened; the car would not start as he tried to leave. It was clear that God intervened because I had just driven the car home and there was nothing wrong with it. I was so thankful and grateful to God, as I walked with Andrew into the house where he managed to calm down. He spent the night on the couch. In the morning, he was feeling much better and I took him back to his father's home. Andrew continued living with his father but he started spending more time at my place. I prayed that he would change his mind and come live with me indefinitely. I started reflecting again about ending my marriage with Sam. It was imperative that I save my son from the anguish of living with his father.

A Warning from the Lord

For anyone who eats and drinks without discerning
the body eats and drinks judgment on himself.
—1 Corinthians 11:29 (ESV)

A few weeks later, on a Saturday morning, I felt the Lord say to me, "What will happen today is not from Me." I didn't understand the meaning of this message; however, I realized it was a warning and it put me on alert. That same morning, while Sam and I were sipping our coffee, he unexpectedly proclaimed, "I have decided to have communion when we go to church tonight. I will just do it."

Well, I was shocked to hear Sam make this statement because every time we went to church, and it was time for communion, he would pass the communion tray along. As he was always adamant about not participating.

During the years I was married to him, he never went to a mosque, yet he would accompany me to church. The days I would arrive home, after a stressful time at the office, he enjoyed reading the Bible to confront me. He also memorized the Lord's Prayer. Despite his interest, he never accepted Jesus as His Lord and Savior; and I never pushed him nor preached to him. I trusted that one day, he would be convinced and would decide to convert, by me being a godly woman and showing him Christ through my actions.

When I asked Sam why he wanted to participate in communion this time, his answer was, "Why not? Am I not worthy of it? I see people doing it all the time and they don't look holy to me, so why shouldn't I?"

These words were not exactly what I was hoping to hear. Usually people are touched by God somehow and seek forgiveness, or seek closeness to God when they make this decision. I now understood clearly what the Lord was trying to warn me about earlier.

I tried to talk Sam out of taking communion. I explained to him that communion was a holy act, a serious act of declaration. That one does it with the right attitude. I also mentioned that it was not wise to challenge God in such a way.

Sam would not listen and asked me why I was not happy on such an occasion. He said, "I thought this is what you have wanted all these years. You should be happy, not upset." I tried to explain to him that I could not be happy for an action taken with the wrong attitude and for the wrong intention. But he insisted that he would do it whether I liked it or not.

At this point, I felt that Sam was crossing a sacred line. My eyes began to open that God may not have been blessing this marriage after all. This was a difficult realization because I had put my well-being into my husband's hands and clung to him for all the comfort he provided. It dawned on me how much I had looked to Sam for physical and emotional comfort. Sure, I worked hard, but Sam made my life away from work, one of ease. My growth in spiritual understanding was showing me that living with faith in God meant having God's blessings over my life. I couldn't imagine living in this world without His blessings for me and my loved ones.

Right now, I was alarmed and puzzled. I had what appeared to me to be a spiritual warning in the morning, and now some bizarre talk from my husband. When we went to church, I wondered if he would go through with his decision. Perhaps he was teasing me? Or he would think it over and change his mind after considering the importance of communion with an attitude of penitence? When the communion tray was passed, Sam grabbed the communion and put it into his mouth, and continued to look at everyone around him, as he chewed with arrogance and pride.

Waiting for a Lightning Bolt to Strike

When we went to bed that night, I could not fall asleep. How could he mock a sacred gift from God? Communion was only offered to believers and was not to be taken lightly or proudly. I kept looking at Sam, wondering if God would just turn him into a little monkey. He was sleeping on his side with his back to me, and then suddenly he turned around. As he was moving, his face turned satanic. It was exactly like the movie *Devil's Advocate* with Al Pacino when the normal faces turn into demonic ones. I never saw such a sight in my life. Horrified, I quickly turned around and instantly heard the Lord say, "Child, stay on this side with Me. Don't worry about him now."

Hearing from God twice in one day, while watching my husband defy God, and then seeing his face turn demonic, made for a long sleepless night. I prayed all night as I knew what had happened today was not good. My biggest challenge was that I was still very much in love with Sam. I was not sure why he decided to take communion but I felt that his insecurities regarding the children, led him to do such a thing. He knew that I always longed for him to accept Jesus as his Lord and Savior. Perhaps, it was a strategic way to appear to be one step closer to accepting Christianity. Maybe he thought I would not leave him now for my children. Instead, I got the shock of seeing him with the face of a demon.

After seeing this horrific creature sleeping in my bed next to me, I knew I had to leave this man. I knew I had to sacrifice my love for Sam and choose God over him this time. I feared and loved God too much and could not stay with Sam, knowing that God must not be blessing our relationship. My heart grew heavy.

When I first married Sam nine years ago, I believed in my heart that God brought him into my life. When Sam found me, I felt that the Lord had sent me a good man to take care of me. I believed that God knew how emotional and vulnerable I was, especially after being married to an emotionless cold-hearted man for thirteen years.

As much as I knew what I had to do, I could not just walk out on Sam. I was too much in love with him. I got on my knees and cried to the Lord. I said, "Lord, if You are not blessing this marriage, then please take this man out of my life, but please do not break my heart."

A Dry Season Sets In

The Lord must have heard my sincere cry. I believe He liked the idea that I was choosing Him over the love of my life. To my amazement, as the days went by, my heart became less warm toward Sam to the point it became dry. This feeling of falling out of love with him was extremely liberating. I had loved this man since I was fifteen. I was addicted to him, yet the Lord hardened my heart over the course of less than six months. Amazingly, I fell out of love with Sam.

By November of that year, I was able to talk to Sam about getting a divorce. I knew he would not understand my spiritual reasoning, so I told him that I could no longer financially support his daughters and his ex-wife. I explained that I did not make enough money to support my children and his children, as they all required more expenses for college. His daughters were attending medical school in Egypt and Andrew was starting to attend university in the United States—I was always financially broke. My bank account, which he managed, was always overdrawn. I further told him that Andrew was miserable living with his father and wanted to move back with me and be close to his sister. But the animosity between Andrew and Sam was preventing him from doing so.

Sam felt betrayed. He kept saying, "I told you, now that you have your children and your health, you do not need me anymore." Even though he was not happy about our plans for a divorce, he agreed to go along with a peaceful, undisputed divorce.

An Amazing Journey Begins

Keep your life free from love of money, and be
content with what you have...
—Hebrews 13:5a (ESV)

Fighting the Flu

I started to feel ill after my company's Christmas party on Dec 6th 2008. I was the one responsible for putting these parties together. Sam usually helped me, especially during these events, but this year Sam was distant. The strain of staying together, despite our amicable agreement to divorce, was showing. At the event, Sam just took to a corner and did not participate at all.

Four days later was my birthday. Sam did not even acknowledge my birthday and ignored me all day long. As the days passed, I started feeling aches and pains throughout my body. The aches were getting worse, and I could not function well at work, so I took some time off to try to get better, but the aches and pains became stronger.

During that time, we managed to go to the courthouse and file for a divorce. The divorce would become final in six months, provided neither party contested the divorce before the six months were up. Sam also requested that I let him stay for three weeks until he could find another place. I agreed as I did not want to throw him out on the streets.

A few days later I woke up with the worst headache I had ever experienced. I could not move my head or even blink without excruciating pain—it felt as if my head was going to explode. This pain continued pounding for several days. I sat at the corner of my couch and was not able to move.

Except for Sam, I was alone. Colleen was away during Christmas break visiting her father and was not due back until January 4th. Sam finally took me to urgent care after I begged him to do so. The doctor did not run any tests on me. He said I must be coming down with the flu, gave me some pain medicine, and sent me home. A few days after starting the painkillers, I felt some relief. Sam also started giving me his blood pressure medicine. This helped to bring down my severe headaches, and I was able to go back to work on Monday, January 5th.

On Friday, January 9th, I had my two cups of coffee and left for work at 7:30 a.m. The traffic was bumper to bumper leading up to my exit off the highway. My favorite Christian radio program was on, but my attention was divided. I had a lot on my mind, and my entire body still ached. I was still worried about catching up on tremendous workload. Critical work projects had fallen behind because of my two weeks of absence.

A Compelling Vision

As I drove, I saw a vision of my brothers and sisters. I had never seen a vision before. In it, one of my family members had just died. I assumed it was my youngest brother Steve, because we had been told by a physician, that people with his condition don't often live past 35 years of age. I interpreted the vision as a warning that he would die soon, so I decided that I must travel to Egypt, as soon as possible, to see him before it was too late.

I instantly remembered how my mom had passed away nine months earlier. I had missed out on saying good-bye because I was not able to take time off of work because of a major project I was overseeing. I had learned a painful lesson by assuming that I could postpone visiting her until a time that would be more convenient for my work. While driving, I was re-living the shame and anger at myself for thinking that her health would wait for my convenience. A few days after I had finished my project, it was her eightieth birthday. I called to surprise her and tell her that I had booked an airline ticket and was flying over to see her. Imagine my grief, as I learned that she had fallen into a diabetic coma that day. She never came out of it. I learned later that she had been calling my name and looking for me in her home, a few weeks prior to her slipping into her coma. The biggest regret in my life was not prioritizing her over my project; hence, missing out on being with her for one last time.

When I arrived at work, my first order of business was to make flight reservations to Egypt to see my brother. I wanted to be with him as soon as possible. I assumed that the vision was a gentle warning from God, so that I would be able to see him before his passing. I called Sam and told him about my decision to go to Egypt immediately. He sounded supportive, "That's fine. Do whatever you have to do. I will still be here when you come back." He was still staying at my place, per our arrangement.

I spent the rest of the day trying to juggle my workload and delegate the remaining projects and tasks. Towards the end of the workday, I had a severe headache. It caused me to lean forward with my elbows on my desk. I held my head as if trying to prevent it from exploding from the pain. A few minutes later, I was overwhelmed with peace. My headache was instantly gone, and I felt compelled to leave. It was almost as though an indescribable force telling me, "Drop everything and go home. Do not think anymore today!"

I left the office and headed towards home. As I drove, I listened to my Christian radio program. The message was about aligning with God and I felt it was speaking to me personally. When I arrived at the parking lot, I remained seated in the dark. I normally would never sit in a parked car in the dark, but I felt compelled to finish hearing the entire message.

A Voice Comforts and Hushes Me!

I finally got out of the car and began walking towards my apartment. As I walked, I heard a clear voice speaking to me. It was not an outside voice, or like an intuition, or a hunch, but a clear voice in my head. To my amazement, I recognized instantly that it was the voice of the Holy Spirit speaking to me clearly, vividly, and softly. I don't really know how I recognized that it was the voice of the Holy Spirit. I never fully understood the concept of the Holy Spirit. I related to Jesus the Son and to God the Father, but could not really grasp the Holy Spirit, so I ignored Him completely all my life. I was not scared once I recognized who He was; rather, I was in awe. We had an interactive dialogue, and it was powerful – a supernatural experience beyond anything words can explain. He stated that He engraved His commandments in my heart since I was born. This was a great revelation because now I understood why I had a compassionate heart. It was nothing of my doing. It was God all along.

This was incredible. This had never happened to me before, and I was in reverence of His presence. I was excited beyond words, wanting to scream and shout to everyone about what was happening. However, He immediately said to me, "Child, you cannot share what you are hearing now with anyone. You must keep your mouth shut!" His words conveyed an image in my mind of His hand covering my mouth as if to tape it shut. *Wow, how can I keep my mouth shut now, Lord?* I thought. This was too exciting to keep to myself, but I kept my mouth shut. I knew I had to obey.

As I walked up to our place, Sam opened the door and asked, "When will you be leaving for Egypt, tomorrow or the day after?"

"I don't know. I cannot think tonight. I will start thinking again tomorrow morning and make a decision then," I said.

"Fine," he said. "Go change and I'll warm up dinner for you."

Colleen came out of her room and gave me a hug and said, "Hey, Mom, how was your day?"

"Exhausting! I can't wait to go to sleep."

"Oh, I'm sorry, Mommy. I love you," she said, as she walked back to her room, where like most teenagers, she spent most of her time and then she closed her door.

I was still in awe as to what was taking place in my mind. I walked to my room to change into more comfortable clothes and went back to the kitchen. Sam had prepared a plate of rice and French green bean casserole for me, which was my favorite dish.

I did not have much of an appetite, so I returned the green beans and just kept the rice on my plate.

As I stood with my back to the refrigerator, holding the plate of rice, I contemplated skipping the rice as well since I had no appetite and the rice appeared too plain. Then I heard the Holy Spirit say, "Child, open the refrigerator. Get plain yogurt and put it on your rice." I was astonished at the attention He gave to such a seemingly trivial matter.

"You care that I put yogurt on my rice?" I asked Him quietly in my mind.

"Child, I am in every little detail of your life."

I was in awe as I realized that He had been in every little detail of my life and I had not even acknowledged Him. I pondered over how I missed out on forty-eight years of knowing Him and making Him a part of my life, while He waited on me *every* minute, as I simply ignored Him. How could that be? I was disappointed in myself for discovering this truth at such a late hour, and I was frustrated at the irony that I could not tell or warn others about what they could be missing. What a shame!

And I will ask the Father, and He will give you another Comforter (Counselor, Helper, Intercessor, Advocate, Strengthener, and Standby), that He may remain with you forever—

(John 14:16, AMPC)

Quiet Fellowship before the Storm

⁷ The earth trembled and quaked,
the foundations of the mountains shook;
they trembled because he was angry.
¹⁶ He reached down from on high
and took hold of me;
he drew me out of deep waters.

—Psalm 18:7, 16 (NIV)

I had no idea what was going to happen to me, nor did I understand why the Holy Spirit had chosen to reveal Himself to me. None of that mattered; all I wanted to do was enjoy His pure, sweet voice and company.

I sat on the couch and ate my plate of rice and yogurt. It is an Egyptian tradition to put plain yogurt on rice. It was my favorite way to eat it and most likely the only way for me to have finished my bowl that evening, which the Holy Spirit obviously wanted me to do. I continued eating while still engaging in a conversation in my mind with Him. I remember He had a great sense of humor, which made me giggle aloud while I ate. Sam immediately asked me if I stopped at a bar and had a drink on my way home. I turned to him and decided to not give him an answer. I did not want to interrupt the amazing dialogue I was having with the Holy Spirit.

When I was done eating, I got up and placed my dish in the sink. I kissed Colleen goodnight then went to my bedroom to brush my teeth and get ready for bed.

As I was lying in bed, I was wondering what was happening to me, and whether I would have time to take care of everything that needed to be done, before I got on the flight to Egypt to see my brother. And then the Lord broke the news to me—my heart dropped to my knees as I heard His words. I don't think any human being is ever ready to hear these words: "Child, it's not your brother—it is you."

I realized that something serious was going to happen to me. Now it all made sense. This was why the Lord revealed Himself to me. I was going to die.

I always assumed that after sleeping through the night I would wake up in the morning. I don't think many of us go to bed wondering whether we will wake up or not the next morning. We always assume life will continue. Now suddenly all the material things in my life did not matter at all. Work and projects did not matter. All that mattered were my loved ones and what kind of impact I had done in their lives. It was not about if I lived enough rather if I loved enough.

Immediately, I thought of poor Colleen, who would wake up in the morning and discover her mom lying dead in bed. My heart was broken over how much pain and devastation my death would bring to my children. It was too overwhelming, and a torrent of tears ran down my face. I wanted to jump out of bed and go hug Colleen one last time. I wanted to call Andrew and say goodbye after telling him how much I loved him, and how much he had been my sunshine, but I could not move—it was too late. I was helpless. The Spirit of Death was upon me as my heart was shattered over my children.

The Lord immediately reminded me of a dream I had experienced three years earlier. In the dream, Andrew and Colleen were walking with Jesus through a meadow. They were on either side of Him with their arms wrapped around His waist. I also had my arms wrapped around Jesus' waist as the four of us walked through this lovely meadow. I was always puzzled about that dream because I could never figure out how the three of us had our arms wrapped around Jesus' waist, and walked by His side without stumbling on each other's feet.

Three years later, the dream finally made sense. I realized that I was walking with them in the meadow, but I was in spirit, not in my body. That was why I did not stumble on their feet. Once I was reminded of that dream, I was at peace with the idea of dying. I realized that the Lord would take care of my children in my absence. He would continue to hold them tight in His arms. Sadly, I told God that I was ok with the fact that I was dying.

I heard the Spirit of God say, "Child, relax! You will be going on a journey, and you will come back and become my ambassador." Wow, those were sweet words to my ears. I let out a sigh of relief and was able to breathe easily again.

Then it dawned on me that I would be an ambassador. My mind started racing and my ego got the better of me. I envisioned myself walking around Times Square with an elongated big head. No one could see me except other ambassadors. Momentarily, I had grandiose thoughts and enjoyed the best title ever: *Ambassador for the Most High God.*

"I am ready, Lord. Where are You taking me? What do I need to do?" I asked Him.

"You need to relax," the Lord responded.

"I am relaxed, Lord. What do I need to do next?" I asked anxiously.

"Child, you need to stop thinking," the Lord said quietly.

I made a big effort to relax, to not think and yet I kept on thinking about whether I was thinking or not. The hardest thing to do was to stop thinking. I kept trying to shut my mind down and kept confusing myself further as I felt the Lord wanting to shout, "Shut your mind *up*, child!" But He was patient with me until I was able to hold my mind still and not think anymore.

"Be still, and know that I am God." (Psalm 46:10a, ESV)

"Shut Your Eyes!"

"Child, you need to shut your eyes. No matter what happens, do not open them. Continue to not think and just relax," the Lord said. I shut my eyes as He asked of me.

"Just remember. No matter what happens, do not open your eyes."

Suddenly an intensely bright light filled the room, as if someone had switched on an amplified light. I was amazed and sensed the presence of the magnificent power of God the Father. There are really no words to describe the presence of that power.

I wanted so much to open my eyes to see Him, but I did not dare defy His orders. This was serious and I needed to obey.

I kept my eyes shut as I heard the windows to my right rattle, as if an earthquake had just started in my room. My heart began racing, faster and faster—so fast that I thought this was how dying from a heart attack must feel. I became terrified and my fear shut the process down. Suddenly, the amplified light was gone, the windows stopped rattling, and my heart beat normally again.

"Oh no," I said to the Lord, as I opened my eyes. "Did I mess up my death? Did I just miss out on it?" I thought I had interfered and that it would pass me by.

"No, child, this one you cannot 'mess up.' You just need to relax more." The soft voice whispered in my mind, as He coached me further. He said, "Shut your mind and stop thinking. I need you to really relax and remember no matter what happens, you must not open your eyes."

I shut my eyes again and tried to relax, as I held my mind still and stopped thinking.

"Do not open your eyes no matter what." He whispered.

The incredible bright light shone again in my room. I immediately felt the presence of God the Father. This time I knew what to anticipate, so I was more relaxed. The windows rattled again. My heart raced like before, but more vigorously. It pounded so fiercely that I felt it was going to explode out of my body. I thought I was going to die now and it was okay. I was not afraid. I felt that the Lord had my back and I was going to be fine no matter what happened. I did not open my eyes, neither did I shut the process down with my fears. I had no fear. I was in total peace, determined to go through the process, even though I knew it meant death. It did not matter anymore, because the Lord was there by my side coaching me step by step. This was exciting! I never imagined that death could be such a beautiful process with the presence of the Lord taking me through it all.

Suddenly, everything became calm again. The bright light was no longer there. The windows stopped rattling and my heart stopped pounding. I was surprised that I was not dead yet.

"Child, consider this next part as an annoyance," the Holy Spirit whispered, as He reminded me of what had happened two days earlier. At that time, I was lying in bed when a chronic abdominal pain suddenly crept up on me. I had a low tolerance for pain due to my fibromyalgia. I wanted to scream, but suddenly I was able to divert the pain. I did this by concentrating on my mind rather than concentrating on my abdomen from where the pain was radiating. I kept doing this exercise and found myself barely feeling the pain, as I controlled it with my brain power—it was a great revelation. I was excited to discover how powerful my mind was. Two days ago, when I made this discovery about the power of the brain, I thought I was brilliant and had discovered something on my own. I had no idea that the Lord was preparing me to cope with severe pain.

"The next step is just an annoyance, child" He repeated. "I need you to concentrate with your mind just like you did two days ago."

Immediately, I felt a whoosh of pain go down both of my legs. I heard the Holy Spirit say, "Child, it is only an annoyance." The pain became stronger and stronger. "It is an annoyance, child," He continued to coach me. I continued to concentrate on what He was saying instead of the pain. The pain became excruciating. It felt like a sledgehammer was breaking my bones. Surprisingly, I was able to endure the pain without groaning or screaming by concentrating on Him and His amazing presence. The pain was strong, but somehow very tolerable. It is hard to explain.

Suddenly, the pain stopped and I sighed in relief—it was over. Then I realized that not only was I not feeling any pain, but I was not feeling anything at all. I felt numb from my head to my toes. I reluctantly asked the Lord, fearing His answer, "Am I paralyzed?"

"Yes, child," He responded in an empathetic voice.

"Nooooo!" I whispered.

"Yes. I'm sorry, child."

"Can I move my legs?"

"No, child"

"Can I at least move my toe?"

"No, child!"

"Can I at least try?"

"Try, child."

I tried to move my toe, but was unable. I had no feeling in my body at all. I was totally paralyzed.

As I lay helpless in my bed, I sensed Sam enter the room. *Great*, I thought. *Now he will realize what happened to me, and he will call 911.* But Sam went over to the other side of the bed, lay down, and went to sleep without acknowledging me.

A Night with the Comforter

I was not able to move, so I stayed on my left side, as the Spirit of the Lord continued to talk with me. It was a beautiful night having the Comforter by my side, keeping me company. It did not matter anymore that I was paralyzed. I did not care whether I would be able to walk again or not. All that mattered was the presence of the Lord with me. *Who am I,* I asked myself, *to be so blessed that the Lord is keeping me company?* I was in so much awe at the whole encounter.

I remember the Holy Spirit going through the Bible and explaining things to me that I had never understood before. His pace was not too fast nor was it too slow—it was perfect. He was also the most perfect teacher, the one you wished you had all throughout school. He even answered all the questions I had wondered about over the years without me asking Him anything at all. I always had questions regarding children suffering around the world and natural disasters—why would God allow such things to happen? He knew all my questions and all His answers made perfect sense, as He revealed them slowly and gently. It is interesting that His answers to these questions are the only parts of my encounter that have been erased completely from my mind. I believe He revealed these answers in order to comfort me at the time, but that they are mysteries that are not meant to be shared or repeated. Thus, He chose to erase them, so I am never tempted to reveal them.

Then I felt the urge to use the bathroom, and I had forgotten that I was paralyzed. After trying to move without any success, I said, "Lord, I need to use the bathroom."

"Go, child," He responded gently.

"Go?," I asked.

"Yes. Go ahead," He said. So, I did. The flow of urine was so much I felt I was going to drown in it.

The Lord revealed to me several visions throughout the night. In one, I was a five-year-old child. I was not a boy or a girl, just a child. Jesus was holding my right hand by His left hand, and He was walking me to my first day in kindergarten. Earlier when he told me that I would be His ambassador, I pictured myself so big and tall. Well, it was humbling to see myself turn into a child in the spiritual world. I was as tall as his knees. I could only see His white robe up to His waist, because from my eye level, His face was not in view.

He walked me into a workshop in an open space. It felt like a carpenter's workshop. Woodworking benches were everywhere. Then Jesus started to play hide-and-seek with me. He hid behind the workbenches, and I could see parts of His face as I ran toward Him, but He would run and hide again.

Then He instructed me to stand on top of a wooden box, which was a type of casket that He placed in front of a tall, large door. He told me not to get off the wooden box and to wait there. He left and I stood there, bored. So, I decided to jump up and down in my spot and turned around in circles, but did not dare get off the box. I kept saying, "I am here! Open the door! I have something in the box for you." But no one opened the door, and I just kept jumping up and down and going around in circles. At the time, I could not understand the entire meaning of this vision except the part about being a child. It made sense that I was only a child in the spiritual world and needed to start in kindergarten, as I had a lot to learn.

The whole night was full of visions as the Holy Spirit did not leave me for one minute. I tried to remember the Holy Spirit's name. I kept saying "Parak... Parakt," but could not quite get it. The sweet Spirit of God said, "Call me Parrot." This was much simpler.

I later found out the name of the Holy Spirit in the Coptic language is *Paraclete* which means *Helper* in the Greek language.

My Eyes Were Shut so I Can See

Even though I walk through the
valley of the shadow of death,
I will fear no evil,
for you are with me;
Your rod and your staff, they comfort me.
—Psalm 23:4 (ESV)

I could feel a soft light penetrating through our bedroom. It was daybreak on Saturday, January 10. I realized the night had passed and I had not died. I did not want my night with the Comforter to end, but I was relieved at the thought that Sam would wake up soon and discover my state, call 911, and rush me to the hospital.

I felt Sam turning around toward me. He put his hand on my shoulder to see if I was awake. I did not respond. He continued to shake my shoulder and call my name: *"Ana, Ana, are you up?"* I did not respond.

He turned my body flat on the bed and kept on shaking me as he called my name. He then opened my right eye with his fingers, looked down on my face and called my name. Then he did the same to my left eye, as I was still not responding but was able to see his face every time he opened an eye. Then he touched my clothes and realized I was soaking wet with urine. "Oh, you peed yourself. We need to get you out of these clothes," he said, as if I was just fine and we were having a normal conversation.

He walked around to my side of the bed, leaned over me and took my gold watch off my wrist. It was an expensive TAG watch. I thought to myself, *why is he taking off my watch instead of calling 911?* Then, he took off my diamond ring and put it away. His actions did not make any sense at all. Next, he opened my lips and tried to put a pill in my mouth, but my teeth were clenched. He kept on trying to squeeze the pill through my teeth, but my jaw would not open and the pill melted against my teeth. It was bitter and tasted like Xanax. Then he put a mint through my lips, which made me wonder how horrible my breath must have been for him to be taking the time to put a mint in my mouth, rather than call 911.

Sam then got onto the bed and pulled my wet clothes off my body. I was now thinking that he was trying to clean me up and dress me in fresh clothes before the ambulance came to take me away. I realized that I must have stunk with all that urine in my hair and on my body.

To my astonishment, Sam climbed on top of my paralyzed body and started raping me. I could not comprehend why he was doing this. Over the years, he and I would always shower and freshen up before we were intimate. He never once attempted to make love to me when I was half asleep or not fresh and fully awake.

After he was done with me, he took a shower, leaving me lying naked and paralyzed in the middle of our bed. He stayed in the shower for about fifteen minutes. Once he was done, he walked towards the bed, and I felt him lean over my body and try to lift me. I could still hear the water running in the shower, but it was a heavier flow this time. It sounded as though he was filling the bathtub for me.

As soon as he tried to move my body off the bed, I fell from his arms onto the floor. He pulled away from my body and said, "I can't carry you. You are too heavy!" Sam left my body curled on the floor in the corner of our bedroom and sat on the bed. *Why is he acting as though all this was normal?*

At this point, I heard Colleen's TV turn on. Her room was right next to ours, and it was Saturday. She woke up and turned on her TV. Sam must have realized that she was up, so he left our bedroom, shut the door, and went to talk to Colleen. Colleen had later told me (after this whole incident) that he had made her breakfast, and when she asked him why I wasn't up making her breakfast instead, he told her that I was very sad over the illness of my brother, so I took a couple of Xanax pills, and went back to sleep, and did not want to be disturbed.

I heard Sam entering our bedroom and felt his body standing over mine. Suddenly, my whole body felt a shock—it felt as though needles were stabbing through my flesh. As I felt the torture of ice water piercing my body, I saw a vision of the Lord Jesus' hand. It was lying on the floor with a big nail being hammered into it. Somehow the pain of the ice water seemed to lessen, as I saw the nail piercing His hand. It is hard to explain, but I was able to endure the pain when I realized how much pain Jesus must have gone through. My pain did not compare to His pain at all.

Sam stopped pouring ice water over me and left the room. I was greatly relieved. He must have been gone for about twenty minutes, and then I heard him come back into the bedroom. I started to wonder what he might do next and wondered why he wasn't calling 911. Before I could finish my thoughts this time, I felt more ice water piercing my flesh. *No, not again! When will this end?* I did not like this at all. It was a torment, but the Comforter was right there telling me, "It will pass, child. It will pass!"

Sam left the room for a while and then came back in and sat on the bed and said to me, "Come on. Enough! If you don't get up, I will call your children to come in and see you naked on the floor."

Why is this man so stupid? I thought. *Can't he clearly see that I can't move? Why is he not calling 911? This does not make any sense. What is he waiting on?*

Weakened, but Not Alone

Then I felt Sam's body leaning over mine and his fingers holding my nostrils shut. I could not breathe. My teeth were clenched. His fingers remained sealing my nose, when suddenly my mouth and jaw opened and I gasped for air. Startled, he released his grip on my nose. He then left the room, leaving me paralyzed, naked, and curled up on the floor.

I suddenly remembered my days when I was going through my deep depression, and I would sit in my office and hold my breath, so I could die. Although I had looked to bring this kind of death on myself back then, I just did not realize it would be so painful.

I was puzzled by Sam's actions. I wondered if he had suddenly decided to suffocate me and finish me off, since I was now paralyzed and useless.

I just did not know what to think anymore, but I never imagined what was happening to me could have been premeditated. I suddenly remembered my million-dollar life insurance policy. Sam was still a beneficiary of half a million dollars, as I had not had a chance to remove him from my policy—it all made sense now.

Sam walked back into the room, and I felt him leaning over my body again. He grabbed my nostrils and held them shut with his fingers, for I don't know how long this time. Suddenly, my mouth opened wide again as I gasped for air. He let go quickly, walked out of the room, and then shut the door.

I was left curled up on the floor, but the Lord was still by my side comforting me. He did not leave me for one second. His presence made all the difference in the world. It did not matter what Sam was doing to me. Having the Lord coach me, step by step, redeemed every passing moment of torture.

I am now convinced that the Lord reveals Himself to each and every victim while they are being tortured. He is a God of love and does not like it when we are victimized. He comes and comforts us during our horrific encounter. He does not save every soul from dying, but He is there to coach and provide peace through it all until He escorts us to the other side. The presence of the Lord takes away any fear and anxiety and eases any pain despite the severity of that pain and torture.

Sam returned to the room and leaned over my body again, but this time he gently covered my mouth with his hand, as he held my nostrils shut with his fingers. I was not able to breathe or gasp for air this time, as his hand remained over my entire mouth, keeping it shut. I felt this was it—I was dying. The suffocation was extremely tormenting until I saw Jesus standing tall. I could not see His face, but I noticed He was wearing a white robe with His right hand stretched toward me. I reached out to Him in my mind, and the pain from the suffocation did not matter anymore. I did not want Jesus to leave without me. I knew that He could stop all of this by removing Sam's hand from gripping my mouth and nose, but I did not want Him to do that—I wanted to go with Jesus.

My Visit to Heaven

*And he said, "Behold, I see the heavens
opened, and the Son of Man standing
at the right hand of God."*
—Acts 7:56 (ESV)

There was no end and there was no beginning. There was no darkness when I stopped breathing. It was as if I took off a heavy coat. I just kept on going.

I could see the sky covered with distinct white clouds, which gently opened, and I saw the most beautiful blue sky. All around it were large animals flying with large wings. The animals had spectacular multiple bright colors. I had never seen animals such as these before in my life. Later, when I saw the movie *Avatar*, I felt that the colorful large flying animals, which were portrayed, reminded me of the same animals I saw flying in Heaven.

I then found myself standing in an open meadow. There was a group of people running around preparing for a wedding. Another group of people were preparing a bride. I was curious to see who the bride was, but I could only see her back and was not able to make it around her to see her face.

I then found myself indoors in a hallway. At one side of the hallway was a majestic chair with an unusually high back. A lady was sitting in it, but I could not see who she was because the chair had a long white veil, which covered her and the chair. I asked someone who was standing nearby who she was. The man told me, "She is the purest of all."

I continued to walk down the hallway, until I came to a door. I saw someone standing at the doorway, whose body was made out of light. It was my mother, Sue. I recognized her soul immediately. Her face had no detail; she was a complete body of light and stood at the same height she had on earth. She greeted me at the entrance of the door. It was beyond overwhelming to see my mother. Somehow, we did not hug but I was experiencing a joy like no other. And then my sister Nadia came towards me to greet me. Nadia looked just like my mother, a body of light, but taller than my mother. Even though I could not see their faces, I recognized their souls right away, and gravitated towards them with the feeling of so much love and incredible joy, which I never before experienced on earth.

It was beyond delight to see my sister in Heaven. I had often wondered if she ever made it there or if she was suffering in Hell, as I was taught by the Church regarding suicide. Seeing my sister in Heaven assured me that the Lord has an immense heart of compassion and mercy and evaluates everyone individually. He must have known how ill she was in her state of depression, and did not count that against her.

Nadia and I left mom in the corridor and went into another room. As we were standing there, I started complaining to Nadia. "I can't handle this joy." I am so overwhelmed I just can't contain it, and I don't know what to do with it." I never thought I would utter these words. I have often been overwhelmed with stress, disappointments and sadness, but never joy.

"With Jesus, things just keep getting better," Nadia said, as she walked me out into the corridor where our mother was still standing. I could not imagine things getting better than this. It was too much already. Then I saw my father walk up and stand next to my mother. I was beyond thrilled and wanted to scream with joy. He was also a body of light, standing taller than my mother but almost the same height as Nadia. I had missed him so much, and just standing there with him, Mom, and Nadia was more than overwhelming. We were communicating, but I am not sure how because we were not talking but we understood each other. And then Nadia said, "Let's go. We have a banquet with Jesus."

I wanted to say, "Come again? With whom?" Oh boy, I was excited! I was going to see Jesus. This was just too much to take in.

My family proceeded to go to the banquet, but somehow, I did not follow them and found myself walking down the hallway again. I came across the majestic chair, but this time it was empty. The white veil was resting on it, but the lady was not there. I asked someone who was standing by the chair "Where did she go?"

"She is running an errand," someone said. *I did not realize they had errands in Heaven,* I thought to myself. I now wonder if they were referring to an errand to Earth.

I kept walking and found myself entering another room. At the end of it, I saw an old man with grey hair. His hair touched his shoulder, but he did not have much of it left. What was interesting was that he was not a body of light; rather, I could see his physical body. I recognized him to be the deceased Pope of the Coptic Orthodox Church, Pope Cyril VI. He was known to be simple, humble, and very compassionate. As I approached him, he questioned, "Where have you been, child?"

"What do you mean?" I asked.

"You haven't been to church," he stated.

"Oh, I am sorry, but I haven't been going to the Coptic Church. I have been going to Calvary Church," I responded.

"Why child?" he asked.

"I found too much judgement and no kindness towards me in the Coptic Church, so I have been going to Calvary instead," I said reluctantly.

"Child, what is your name?" he asked, but with a tone indicating he already knew.

I told him my given name.

"What does it mean, child?" Again, it sounded like a rhetorical question.

"It means *compassion*," I said.

"You are looking for compassion child, but you are what we need inside our church, child. Hurry up back, child. There is not much time left," he said, as he rushed me out.

I can't remember where I went next, whether I was standing or sitting down. Suddenly, I saw the face of Jesus revealing itself to me. I first saw His forehead and then gradually His eyes were revealed—I was speechless. His face continued to be revealed. I could slowly see His long nose as it took longer to reveal. I could not help myself when I said, "You are Jewish, aren't you?" Jesus gently smiled. Then His mouth and chin were revealed, and I saw His whole face. I was in awe. Just in awe. His face was glorious!

He was not as handsome as I imagined or as He was portrayed in movies. His eyes were dark brown and His complexion was olive. His face was more rugged than I expected. I felt bad knowing that He could read my thoughts; I did not want to offend Him by thinking He was not as handsome as I expected.

I later read in the Old Testament that Isaiah described Him not to be handsome:

> *...he had no form or majesty that we should look at him, and no beauty that we should desire him.*
>
> (Isaiah 53:2b, ESV)

This description now made sense to me because if Jesus were a handsome man, as He was portrayed in the movie *Jesus of Nazareth*, there would be a risk that women whom were vulnerable during His time, could have been attracted to Him as a man rather than to His purity and holiness.

I often look back on my encounter and ask, "Who sees Jesus' face and utters a question like the one I uttered to Him?" There are songs that ask what a person would do or say when he or she sees Jesus' face, and none of them mention asking Him if He was Jewish.

A Sudden Return

I had travelled outside of time. I don't know how I know this because I have never comprehended the notion of a place which stood outside of time, yet everything was clear to me about what had just taken place.

It was late afternoon when I was suddenly looking down at a flow of traffic on a busy, bustling freeway. The world looked exceptionally dry compared to where I had just been. Soon after, I found myself in my room, looking down on my bed, where Sam lay holding my lifeless, naked body in his arms. I saw it from above, as if I were a bystander.

Abruptly, I jumped from his arms and stood up at the foot of the bed—I was no longer paralyzed. As a matter of fact, I was filled with strength and amazing energy. I wish I would have had a camera to capture the look on Sam's face, which conveyed a mixture of disbelief and confusion. He was stunned and did not know what to do. I noticed that I could not speak. I had no voice. I started making strong gestures at him, indicating to him to get out of the house. He just stared at me and his confusion narrowed to a smile, as he said, "Calm down and come back to bed."

But that was the last thing I was going to do, and I continued gesturing to him to leave.

"I am not going anywhere," he said.

I showed him with my gestures that I saw how he tried to suffocate me and how disgusted I was with him. What was strange was that I was still naked while doing this, and that did not bother me. I was not embarrassed at all, considering I am a reserved, conservative woman. I am undressed only behind a closed door. I never allowed Sam to see me naked unless we were intimate and the lights were dimmed low. The fact that I was not embarrassed about my nakedness, made me believe that I was still somehow in the Spirit and was back temporarily to say good-bye to Colleen, and to scare the daylights out of Sam. I also wanted to be sure to leave a trail for the police, so he would not get away with trying to murder me and cash out my life insurance.

Then I started pacing back and forth, in front of the bed, with my hands held tightly behind my back, the way my father used to pace. I had a lot of energy and I was looking at Sam with anger. I then gestured to him to ask him if he knew who I was. He responded with hesitation and fear in his voice, "Uncle Mo?" I have no idea how this happened, but this is my father's name, and Sam recognized him in my body. I know it sounds eerily strange, but somehow Dad's spirit must have been able to come down with me to help deal with this horrible man.

Sam was scared and annoyed because I kept insisting that he leave, and I refused to get back into bed with him. Then he started threatening that if I did not relax and calm down, he would do something to Colleen.

As soon as Sam mentioned Colleen, I became furious. After what I witnessed him do to me, I realized I was dealing with a criminal and wanted to protect my daughter. I still could not speak, so I gestured with a furious angry look to let him know that he had better not even think of harming my daughter. I stood at the door of our bedroom and forbade him to leave our room, as I could hear Colleen still watching TV in her room.

Sam pushed me out of the way, opened the door, and walked into Colleen's room, as he yelled something to her. I followed him not caring that I was still naked, thinking that Colleen would not see me since I was still in the Spirit.

The Table Turns: This Way and That

Colleen was sitting on her bed doing her homework while watching her TV. She jumped off her bed as soon as she saw me walking behind Sam naked.

"Mom! What's wrong?" she said.

I ran back to my room as soon as I realized that Colleen could see me. She ran into my room after me, so I asked her to close the door quickly before Sam followed us back. She did and managed to lock it immediately. She then quickly got my robe and put it around my body. As soon as Colleen held me in her arms, I realized that I was able to speak again. She had heard me when I asked her to close the door!

Sam started knocking, but I instructed Colleen not to open the door. Sam knocked even louder and yelled, "Open the door or I will break it down!"

Poor Colleen looked confused and could not figure out what was going on. I must have looked horrible. My hair was so frizzled and messed up after being soaked with all that water and urine. My sweet journey with death had also enhanced the grey in my hair, so there was grey everywhere even though I was only forty-eight.

I did not want to scare Colleen, but I wanted her out of the house and away from any danger. I did not know what this man was planning next and wanted to avoid putting her in harms way. Furthermore, I was not sure if I was going to die or what exactly was going to happen to me, and I did not want her to watch me die or witness anything more traumatic than what she had already experienced. Sam stopped banging on the door and went away. I reassured her that I was fine and just needed some rest. I convinced Colleen to go to church with her friends, as there was always a youth meeting on Saturdays. Colleen's church friends picked her up shortly afterward.

After Colleen left, I was not afraid of Sam and did not feel I needed to lock my bedroom door anymore. Sam calmly entered the room and lay down on the bed. I asked him to leave, but he insisted on staying. I was still not sure what would happen next but assumed that I was just temporarily back on earth and would be leaving again soon. I decided to take this opportunity to speak to him about Jesus. I felt this could be my last task before leaving.

I sat on the edge of the bed where he was laying, and I held onto a Bible in one hand and a large wooden cross in the other. At first, Sam refused to listen, so I became firm and instructed him to listen for his sake. I explained the Trinity and how it relates to God the Father, Jesus the Son, and His Holy Spirit. I remembered he never understood why God would let His Son die on the cross for us.

I told him that I may be going away soon, and he would never see me again. As soon as I mentioned that I would be going away, his facial expression changed and he said in a firm tone, "Ana, WE will never leave you!" His usage of the word "we" made me realize that there was no sense in talking with this man anymore. I became aware that he was being used by an evil power, which I was now against. This was a higher spiritual battle that I was not sure I could handle.

At this point, I knew I needed to get away from him, so I walked into the master bathroom and for some reason I did not feel the need to close the door. I was not afraid of him. I was surrounded by peace and knew that I was protected by a higher power.

I sat on the bathroom floor leaning on the vanity as I held onto my cross and hugged my Bible tightly against my chest. Somehow Sam was not able to follow me into the bathroom. He was pacing back and forth outside of it, but could not enter. It was as if the bathroom was my sanctuary; protection from him. I sat on the floor until I dozed off.

I woke up to the soft touch of Colleen's hands. She was kneeling in front of me, as I sat curled on the floor. She embraced me tightly, and asked, "Are you all right, Mom?"

I smiled with joy at seeing my baby again and asked her to take me to her room. Sam was in the living room watching TV, as Colleen and I walked to her room and closed the door quickly.

Colleen brought me water and gave me bread she brought from church. I was hungry, as I had not eaten since the bowl of rice Sam had given me twenty-four hours ago. Again, I was so worried about Colleen and did not want her to see me die. I was not sure what was going to happen to me—it was very confusing. I was still not sure if I had come back temporarily and was going to die again. I felt the most important task was to get her out of the house and away from any harm or trauma that may be approaching. I convinced her that I needed to visit my sick brother in Egypt for two weeks and that she needed to go spend those two weeks with her dad and brother.

While she packed, Colleen called her father to come and pick her up. When Paul and Andrew arrived, they called her to let her know that they were waiting for her in the parking lot. Once I learned that they were there, I told Colleen to have her dad call the police because Sam had tried to kill me. Colleen was hesitant and did not want to do so. She told me that I was just tired and there was no way Sam would have tried to kill me because he loved me so much and was always so considerate and understanding. I insisted that she ask her dad to call the police—she finally did.

Side-Lined!

But I am like a deaf man; I do not hear,
like a mute man who does not open his mouth.
—Psalm 38:13 (ESV)

I stayed with Colleen in her room until the police arrived. Andrew, who was waiting in the car with his father, came up to the apartment when he saw the police arrive. Sam opened the door and let everybody in. I came out of Colleen's room and was happy to see Andrew. The police officers asked me what had happened. I proceeded to tell them that my husband tried to kill me. I noticed that both Andrew and Colleen's facial expressions were full of disbelief, as I explained what had happened. They were shaking their heads in doubt. They had never received reports of Sam and I arguing or fighting. All they saw in the past was complete harmony and how Sam always treated me with love and respect.

The police officers noticed the doubt on my kid's faces, and I could tell they, as well, did not believe me. I learned later that when Paul initially called the police, he told them, "my ex-wife must have lost her mind and is claiming that her new husband tried to kill her."

Paul had always claimed that I was not mentally or emotionally fit to raise our children during our custody battles and saw this as an opportunity to get Colleen back.

The police officers questioned Sam, who was very relaxed as he expressed his love for me and how he would never hurt me.

He acted very concerned about my condition, as tears ran down his face. I told the police officer that we had filed for a divorce a few weeks earlier, which Sam denied. The officers asked to see the divorce papers, but when I went to my room to retrieve them from my desk, they were no longer there. I couldn't prove anything, since I was no longer paralyzed and there were no apparent signs of abuse.

I was astonished that no one believed me. I was amazed at how smoothly Sam acted and how quickly everyone was ready to write off the situation as another emotional, hysterical woman having a mental breakdown. They suggested that they could call the paramedics for me for a physical evaluation.

The paramedics arrived after the children left with their father. Several men came into my bedroom and checked my vital signs. All my vitals were good, my blood pressure and sugar levels were perfect, despite me being a diabetic. One of the men kneeled on the floor in front of me, as I sat on the side of the bed. He asked me to pull on his fingers very hard, and I pulled his entire body forward. Usually, I am more on the weak side, but that particular night I was extremely strong.

"This woman is as strong as a horse," he reported to the other paramedics.

Sam told them that I must have had a nervous breakdown because of my heavy workload at the office. He also added that I was very disturbed over the sickness of my younger brother who may be dying overseas. He told them I had taken several medications to calm down.

The officers and paramedics did not know what to do with me; they could not find anything wrong. They asked if I wanted to stay at home or be taken to the hospital for further evaluation. I could not believe that no one believed me. They were about to leave me alone with the man who had just tried to kill me.

I got dressed quickly and asked to be taken to the hospital when I realized that they were not going to arrest Sam. They placed me on a gurney and pushed me towards the ambulance. I noticed Paul and the kids were still in the parking lot, waiting in the car. I hoped that they would follow the ambulance to the hospital that night.

Unfortunately, they didn't. Sam, however, did follow the ambulance.

I was taken to a hospital and was put under continuous supervision. A female nurse spent the night at my bedside. She was a sweet girl with a great sense of humor. She asked me where I was from and I answered, "I am Coptic." I am not sure why I said that. I never refer to myself as being Coptic. I usually say I am Egyptian or Canadian. She downloaded hymns and songs from a Coptic Orthodox site, and played them all night long for me. I hadn't heard Coptic songs for quite some time, and hearing them brought me so much peace that night. This sweet girl kept me entertained all night long by chatting and sharing her adventurous stories with me.

Then I saw Sam in the hallway outside my room; he was dressed in a suit. I told the nurse that I didn't want him anywhere near me. She didn't let him enter my room, so he kept pacing in the hallway, staring at me as he walked by every few minutes.

In the morning, a lady who said that she was a social worker came to see me.

"Ma'am, do you know why you were brought in here?" she asked.

"Yes, my husband raped me and tried to kill me," I answered. She left my room, as I dozed off.

I woke up startled by a loud, deep voice saying, "Ma'am, we have to ask you some questions." A tall, Caucasian, heavy set man, in a police uniform, stood by my bed.

"Can you please lower your voice? You startled me," I said. He gave me a dirty look, as I must have embarrassed him in front of the doctor and nurse who were also in my room. I found out later that he wrote in his report that I had assaulted a police officer.

After the policeman left my room, I was moved on a gurney into an ambulance. It turned out that my new destination was a mental hospital.

A Season Among the Mad

I was in an ambulance being driven around for what may have been hours. The first hospital in Orange County had no beds available, so the ambulance continued on to LA County. The intake person at the next hospital asked me several questions, one of which was, "Where are you from?"

"I am Coptic," I responded once again.

I have no idea why I would say that I was Coptic. This is not even a nationality, but somehow this is how I identified myself, as if I had just discovered my roots when I visited Heaven and felt that this, above all else, was who I was.

Another question I was asked was, "Who is your employer?"

"SSI," I responded.

The man questioning me gave me a confused look. I later found out that he assumed I was referring to the Social Security Insurance office, which shares the same acronym. This explains why I was admitted to their ICU section of the hospital where they place highly disturbed mental patients.

During my first night at the hospital, a male nurse came into my room and gave me some pills to take.

"What are you giving me?" I asked.

"This is your medication," he responded.

"I understand, but I want to know exactly what it is," I said.

"Ma'am, the doctor ordered these medications for you to take," he said.

"I would like to know what medication he is giving me because I don't usually take any medication before I sleep," I said softly.

"Ma'am, you need to cooperate," the nurse said firmly.

"I want to cooperate, but was just wondering what you are giving me," I said quietly.

"Ma'am, are you refusing to take your medication?" he asked with an even firmer tone.

"I just want to know what you are giving me," I continued.

"Well, ma'am, you don't have to take your medication. I cannot force you to take it," he said.

"Great, then I don't want to take it, as I don't feel I need anything right now," I said.

"Okay, then I will just let your doctor know that you are not cooperating," he stated, as he walked out of the room.

I woke up and found myself in a room with three beds where other women were sleeping. My bed was next to a window. In another bed was a young lady who cried most of the time. She appeared to be no more than eighteen years old. In the bed closest to me, was an older woman in her mid-fifties who lay moaning from aches in her body. She was so thin that her bones ached from lying on the excessively thin, hard mattress.

I followed everyone to a large hall where they were serving breakfast. There was a long line formed at a table, which had three large coffee dispensers. Strangely that morning, I could not tolerate the smell of coffee and found myself walking past the table. I usually can't function without my coffee, and rush to get my first cup, as soon as I open my eyes in the morning. Somehow, my spirit was repelled from the smell of it, and I did not want to go even near that table.

After breakfast, the doctor asked to see me. I remember his deep-blue eyes. He was a Caucasian man in his mid-fifties. "I understand that you are refusing to take your medication, Ms. Christina," he said. All I did was stare at his beautiful blue eyes and did not say a word.

"Ms. Christina, do you understand that if you refuse to cooperate, I cannot send you home?" he said.

Again, I just stared at his deep-blue eyes and did not respond. I was afraid to say the wrong thing. I felt that all my words were being monitored and I was scared of making things worse. So, I decided to stay silent.

"Okay, Ms. Christina, you can go now," the doctor said.

The doctor did not send me home, and I remained in the ICU section, which had many troubled people. Many patients were yelling and screaming and using foul language. I remember one man enjoyed taking off his pants and running down the hallway half-naked.

The hospital had once been an elementary school and was now horribly run down. The toilets were plugged and smelled offensive. I had to wait a few days for my turn to take a shower. The attendant told me that I should soap up my body first, before turning on the water, because there was not enough water. I went in a single shower room and did as she said, but when I turned the shower on, no water came out. The shower was broken and they did not have the decency to put a sign indicating that it was out of order. I had to wipe the soap off my body and get dressed without taking a shower. The two other showers were broken as well. The employees were rude and treated us with no respect or dignity. They looked down on us and had no sense of compassion or empathy. They did not care for our wellbeing, and it was obvious they did not realize nor care about how vulnerable some of us were. The environment was disturbing and chaotic, but I kept my quiet demeanor and stayed focused on the Lord in order to not lose my peace.

I saw things and events one would never imagine could still be going on in this day and age in a hospital setting. It was an unusual experience, and it is hard to write about it because of how disturbing it was. It is sad how these places are so chaotic. Some patients whom are admitted would definitely become more disturbed after spending a few days there.

I remember they took my reading glasses from me and locked them up with my belongings because in a mental hospital they assume a patient may try to hurt themselves and use the glass, of the eye glasses, to cut themselves. The first night there, I found a bible in the drawer next to my bed, so I opened it while I laid there before I went to sleep. I was not sure how I was going to see the words without my reading glasses. To my surprise, I found the words magnified in 3D and were raised towards me—I could read them very clearly. Not sure how that happened, but I was amazed and felt very blessed that I was able to read the bible before I went to sleep.

In all this chaos, the Lord used me as a vessel for His good work in that place. I witnessed warfare between evil and good spirits. I realized that mental hospitals are a draw for the devil. Most people in these hospitals are depressed and confused, and evil spirits prey on them to make them feel more worthless and suicidal. But I also witnessed how the Lord has His full armor in these places and protects the weak.

Patients were drawn to me even though I was hardly speaking. Every evening one of the ladies would come up to my bed and ask me to pray for her. Unfortunately, as soon as I start praying slowly with someone, a supervisor would come and interrupt us and say to me that patients are not allowed to come close to one another or sit on the side of someone else's bed. They would not listen or make any exceptions even after I explain that we were simply praying. They always had to interrupt and send the other patient back to their bed crying.

Truth Prevails, Some Help at Last

Seven days passed before I was told that I would attend a hearing where a judge would determine if I was being kept against my will. On that day, I was directed to a small room where a

Caucasian gentleman introduced himself as a judge. A young lady was also present and introduced herself as a patient advocate. The judge appeared to be a stern, older man. I was so afraid to say anything that could be misunderstood. And then I noticed that he was wearing an off-white tie with dark-gray crosses. The crosses on his tie comforted me. I felt it was a message from the Lord reminding me that He is in control and not to be afraid. I then felt that it was okay to talk.

One of the questions the judge asked me was how much I made per week. I remember the puzzled look on his face when I stated my weekly salary.

"Do you make this amount per month?" he asked.

"No, per week," I stated.

"Where do you work?" he asked with a confused tone.

"At SSI," I said.

"You mean you collect that much for disability?" he asked.

"No, what disability? I am paid by a company named SSI."

"What do you do for SSI?" he asked, still puzzled.

"I am their Chief Financial Officer," I answered.

The judge and the patient advocate both looked at each other, as they realized something in my records was wrong.

"But it says here you are collecting Social Security from SSI," he stated.

"No, I work for SSI. It's a food distributing and manufacturing company," I said.

The judge looked at the patient advocate with confusion and concern.

"It says here that when you were admitted, that you were saying you were Jesus coming to save the world. Do you remember saying these words?" the young lady asked.

"No way. I am Christian, but I know I am not Jesus," I responded with a smile.

"Could it be that you were praying out loud and they misconstrued what you were saying and recorded it wrong?" she continued.

"That is possible," I said.

I later learned that Sam told them at the hospital that I was running around saying I was Jesus coming to save and heal the world.

"Can you tell us what happened before you were admitted?" she asked.

I told them that my husband tried to kill me and asked them if they could report him to the police and have a restraining order placed against him. Only after he left my place could I go home. They responded that they were not able to do such proceedings on my behalf, and I would need to pursue this when I left the hospital.

A few hours after my hearing, I was transferred to another unit in the hospital. It was a much calmer unit that attended to patients with depression. Two days later, my sister Mira, who lived in North Carolina was finally able to locate me. She immediately flew in with her husband and came to visit me at the hospital. They brought Andrew and Colleen with them.

Apparently, it was difficult for my family to find me. Sam did not tell them where I was at first. The first hospital did not release any information to my family either. They would not tell them that I was transferred to a mental hospital. Sam eventually told my family that I had a nervous breakdown, and I had been admitted to a mental hospital for observation.

I was so thrilled to see my son and daughter. Andrew and Colleen were so relieved to know that I was not dead, nor had I become permanently insane. Their father told them that I had lost my mind and would never be the same again.

The doctor released me once he found out I had a safe family member, my sister, who could sign me out and take me home.

As soon as we arrived home, my brother-in-law changed the locks. Two hours later, we heard Sam at the door trying to enter with his old keys. My brother-in-law opened the door to greet him, and Sam was in shock to find us all at home.

We all sat down in the living room, and my sister asked Sam why he did not call 911, as soon as he realized something was wrong with me.

"I was trying to revive her before the ambulance would arrive," he responded.

"Why would you shut my mouth and nose?" I asked as I choked up with tears.

"I was trying to make you alert," he said.

None of what he said made any sense. When my sister and brother-in-law saw how emotional I was getting. They convinced him that he needed to move out for a few days until I felt better. Once I felt better, we would all talk about what happened. They gave him money to book a hotel room. Sam packed his things and left, and I never allowed him back in my home.

Both Andrew and Colleen came to stay with me while my sister and her husband were there. Being among family again was such an awesome feeling. I realized I was not going to die, and I was back with my loved ones.

I did not mention to anyone about my spiritual encounter while Sam was finishing me off. I realized that just saying that he tried killing me had made me sound irrational, and I was locked up as a result of it. Can you imagine what would have happened if I had said that I visited Heaven and had seen my mom and dad? I think I would still be locked up to this day!

Another Dark Twist of Lies

Two days later, I received notice from my lawyer that Paul showed up in court with an ex-parte notice claiming that I was a desperately sick woman and mentally unstable. I was allegedly walking around the house naked all the time, and I was admitted to a mental hospital; thus, I was not fit to care for my daughter Colleen. My lawyer did not check her voice mail and missed hearing the notice that she had to appear in court on my behalf. Hence, she did not show up in court to fight these false allegations. The judge awarded Paul full custody of Colleen effective immediately, and I was only allowed to see her under supervision. Colleen later told me that when she had to go back and live with her dad, it felt like she had been sitting comfortably in first class but then suddenly snatched and then found herself in cargo.

Losing custody of Colleen after all this was more devastating than being tortured and left for dead—it felt like my heart was literally torn away from me. It was one of the most difficult heartaches I had ever felt—I could not stop crying. I could not believe Colleen was being taken from me when I needed her most. I knew Paul was vindictive, but did not think that he would do something so manipulative and hit me below the belt at such a fragile time. He capitalized on this moment. He had always claimed that I was mentally unstable and an unfit mother, and now he had circumstances to use to his advantage.

Instead of pursuing Sam and having him held accountable for what he tried to do to me, I put all my energy into trying to regain custody of Colleen. I knew I had to prove that I did not just flip out, lose my mind, and decide to walk around the house naked.

I had to prove that I was a victim of an attempted murder, but it was not going to be easy to prove this because I was no longer paralyzed and there were no witnesses to Sam's actions.

At first, I assumed that Sam was tempted to finish me off after I became paralyzed. Of course, the incentive of inheriting half a million dollars from my life insurance made the temptation stronger. I started by trying to figure out what caused me to become paralyzed in the first place. I went for several tests to see if I had suffered a heart attack or a stroke, but both tests were negative. My sister left after my brother Fred flew in to stay with me. I shared with him what took place during my episode. Once I mentioned that Sam raped me while I was paralyzed, Fred suspected that this was a premeditated murder.

After more detailed analysis of the whole episode, we both concluded that Sam was not just trying to finish me off once he realized that I was paralyzed; rather, he must have caused me to be paralyzed with the intention to murder me. The act of raping me before killing me was to prove that we were intimate and to drive away any notion that we were getting a divorce or that there was any hostility between us.

I hired another family lawyer and went to court over Colleen's custody and the ex-parte order. We could not obtain any evidence to prove to the judge that I did not lose my mind due to a nervous breakdown. When my lawyer mentioned in court that my husband tried to kill me, Paul's lawyer laughed, which made the judge chuckle as well—I was being mocked. The judge ordered that my mental state be evaluated by a psychiatrist for six more months while Colleen continued to live with her father.

Following the Science

I was broken and devastated, as I walked out of the courtroom. My lawyer suggested that I should do a forensic hair analysis to find out exactly what caused my paralysis. It did not matter that two months had passed since my incident.

I followed my lawyer's advice and submitted a hair sample to an independent lab for forensic analysis. I have been bleaching my hair with blonde highlights for the last twenty years. After my incident, I had too much grey showing at the roots and needed to get my hair highlighted and colored again. This time, Colleen convinced me that I should not highlight my hair with bleach because she missed my darker color. So, we went to the store and picked up an over - the- counter color. We returned home and she colored my hair for me. I usually would never agree to such a request. I was not used to having darker hair, but thank God I went along with her and listened to her wishes. My hair needed to be unbleached for this test to work. If I had bleached my hair, it would have been ineligible for the test and may have never known what caused my paralysis.

The lab results were given to a doctor who prepared a letter addressed to the family court, stating what the analysis had revealed. His letter stated the following:

> I have received lab reports which indicate very high amounts of several heavy metals on her hair analysis, consistent with toxicity, possibly induced by poisoning. These abnormalities include a Mercury level which is 60 times the reporting limit, Selenium 69 times the limit, Antimony 49 times the limit, Lead 280 times the limit, Bismuth 40 times the limit, and most disturbing, Barium at 2750 times the limit. The symptoms she described which were present at the time of her psychiatric hospitalization in January and thought to be psychotic in nature were consistent with toxicity due to Barium or perhaps Mercury.

These lab results made sense. "The uptake of very large amounts of barium that are water-soluble may cause paralysis and in some cases death," stated the report on the chemical properties of barium under "Health and Environmental Effects."

According to the Agency for Toxic Substance and Disease Registry, "The predominant effect following ingestion of high doses of barium is hypokalemia which can result in ventricular tachycardia, hypertension and/or hypotension, muscle weakness, and paralysis."[1]

Another website[2] lists the following information on barium poisoning:

> "When barium accumulates in the body, it usually affects the functions of the nervous system. Barium poisoning displays symptoms that are similar to flu, which is why it is not strange to find the condition misdiagnosed as flu."

How could I have such a large amount of barium showing up in my hair analysis? Wouldn't I know if I had been poisoned? Research showed that barium has no color, no taste, and no smell. I usually ate at home and Sam usually prepared my food.

I realized that Sam could have been putting poison in my cup of coffee before he served it to me every morning since early December after I told him that I wanted to divorce him. He would bring my coffee to me in bed, as I opened my eyes.

When I became worried about my younger brother Steve and decided to drop everything and go visit him in Egypt, Sam must have realized that he needed to finish me off that night before I traveled. He must have also realized that he was running out of time, because I only agreed for him to stay at the apartment for

---

three weeks, after we filed for divorce. He must have put a heavy dosage of poison in my rice that night.

Him raping me while I was paralyzed, now made more sense because he needed to show that we were on good terms before I died, as we had just been intimate. His plan must have been to place me in the bathtub and claim that I overdosed on Xanax, fell asleep in the bathtub, and simply drowned.

Some Justice Among More Injustice

Around the end of March that year, I went to the local Police Station with the lab reports in the hopes that they would open my file and initiate a thorough investigation of what took place. I felt that the lab report proving a heavy dosage of different poisons, along with Sam's name as a beneficiary to my million-dollar life insurance, would indicate that he had enough motive to try and kill me.

To my surprise, they were not interested. They sent me away and said that a detective would call me. After an entire week passed, I received a call from one of their detectives, who asked me if I had a videotape proving that Sam put poison in my coffee or food. I could not believe she expected me to have a video camera filming what Sam was doing. She explained that they needed proof that he was the one administering these chemicals. I asked her to speak to Colleen directly, that she would be able to tell her point of view of the events, which took place that day, and would back up my story. The detective called Colleen. She answered her phone while sitting next to her dad in his car. The detective failed to ask Colleen if this was a good time to talk. Colleen was terrified of her dad and was unable to respond properly to the detective's questions because she did not want her dad to know that she was talking to the detective regarding the incident. I later received a call from the detective advising me that I should keep a diary from this day forward in case Sam tried to hurt me again. She did not feel it was necessary to meet with me to discuss anything further, and she closed the case.

It did not make any sense to me that the Police Department would not be interested in investigating this attempted murder, until I read an article in the county newspaper. It was written on June 17 2009 (same year as my encounter) entitled: "IF IT'S AMERICA'S SAFEST CITY, IT MUST BE CENTERVILLE" The article stated the following: "...Centerville in 2008 once again had the lowest number of crimes per capita in the country for any city with more than 100,000 people." Another article in the same newspaper dated November 23rd, 2009, listed the very city, where I was hospitalized and interrogated by the police officer, before he sent me away to a mental hospital, as the third safest city in the nation, and the city of Centerville ranked fourth in the nation.

I often wonder if they avoided investigating my case to preserve Centerville's reputation and ranking.

I did not want to rock the boat and pursue a restraining order against Sam. The divorce we filed in late December would become final after a six-month cooling-off period, as long as neither of us canceled it. I felt that I needed to wait out the six months without provoking him, and giving him a reason to cancel the divorce.

Unfortunately, Sam canceled the divorce in May before the six months were up. I now had nothing to lose, so I hired a lawyer and filed for a restraining order against him. At the hearing, the lady judge empathized with Sam and felt he must not be that dangerous since I waited so long to file a restraining order. After all this man did to me, I was denied a simple restraining order against him. Ironically, I was awarded a restraining order ten years prior when I was able to prove that Paul merely threatened to kill me. Apparently, over the years the use of restraining orders had been abused, causing judges to become more reluctant to issue them, even when they are needed.

The hearing in family court regarding Colleen was in September. The lab reports were more than enough to prove to the judge that I was a victim of foul play, and I was awarded back full custody of Colleen. That was the happiest day of my life.

I didn't want to be anywhere near Sam, but he was still driving a car that was in my name. I tried to get him to pay for the monthly payment, but he wouldn't. One day, he drove up to me when I was crossing the street around my apartment, rolled down the window and said, "I just want to tell you that if you try to take this car from me, I will run you over and hurt you in the middle of the day, and I will get away with it because no one will believe you."

I quickly went back upstairs, called the police and reported the new threat. The police officer awarded me a temporary restraining order.

I went to court ten days later to convince a judge that I needed a permanent restraining order. Sam showed up in court and told the judge that I tried obtaining a prior restraining order against him, and it was denied by another judge. He claimed I was lying and that we were just having marital disputes. Again, I was denied a simple restraining order.

Several months passed without hearing from Sam, until one day I received a call from him. He stated he was leaving the country, and if I wanted my car, I was to meet him at a Starbucks later that day. I contacted a friend to accompany me and went to Starbucks that same night. I did not know what to expect. He gave me the keys, said goodbye, and wished me luck with my life. He left in a car driven by another man.

Sam was never held accountable for what he did. With the grace of God, I divorced him in February, four years after we had remarried. He left the country soon after and remains far away to this day!

Although One Comes Back from the Dead...

"And he said, 'No, father Abraham, but if someone goes to them from the dead, they will repent.' He said to him, 'If they do not hear Moses and the Prophets, neither will they be convinced if someone should rise from the dead.'"
—Luke 16:30–31 (ESV)

Years have passed since my encounter with death. As you can imagine, I have asked myself many questions. I have been slow to speak. There is much to wonder about. The Lord has since put it in my heart to share my story with others, but most of all to tell about the communion with the Holy Spirit.

I ponder my time in Heaven and the details of my experiences and what they meant. Spending time with my parents and sister whom appeared to me as beings of light, was more than comforting, especially the assurance that my sister Nadia is in Heaven. Watching Jesus reveal Himself to me was breathtaking, but the most remarkable realization was when the Comforter told me that He is in every little detail of my life.

Speaking the Truth

Many people have been inspired by my story. Some have been shocked as they were not prepared to hear about such a frightening experience; especially people at church. Therefore, I have learned to warn people about the subject matter of my story, so they can choose to hear my message or not.

In one instance, a young woman questioned how clear my head could have been during the attack, since I had most likely been poisoned. She assumed my visions and the voices I heard were hallucinations. I cannot blame those who hear the story, for being cautious. After all, even my own family and those who were supposed to help me, including the police and doctors, were doubtful and skeptical. They felt that I was at least confused, if not paranoid, and out of touch with reality.

My answer to those who doubt my story is that it's common sense—what I experienced was real and is documented. I have the doctor's report that shows evidence of the poisoning. This was sufficient for me to regain custody of my daughter. More important is my sudden return to health. If I were merely hallucinating due to the poison and had a dream, then I would have remained paralyzed when I awoke. But one moment I was ill and completely paralyzed, and then suddenly I jumped from Sam's arms, fully well and "as healthy as a horse," as the paramedic put it. I had no sign of weakness, poisoning, paralysis, or even issues about my diabetes. The poison that had paralyzed me, had been defeated completely and instantly, proving that something miraculous had taken place.

The comfort and peace I felt during the attack was so precious and allowed me to endure the suffering and pain. I felt assured that we are never left alone when we are persecuted, tortured, or when we endure a tragic death. People who lose a loved one, especially a child, to a horrific death, are often tortured the rest of their lives, re-living their child's fear and pain in their last moments. I am assured that the Holy Spirit was with them, comforting, easing their pain and suffering, while coaching them step by step, as He gently escorted them to Heaven.

I often wondered about the pain my father must have suffered during his tragic car accident. I used to break down and cry hard just thinking of it. Now I have comfort knowing that the Lord must have been with my father and helped him endure the blow to his head, that made a hole through his skull. Now I have closure and peace.

I have forgiven Sam for what he did. I hold no bitterness over what happened. As a matter of fact, I am delighted that by his evil actions, I had the opportunity to have an encounter with the Lord. I discovered the joy of living and acknowledging the Holy Spirit in every remaining part of my life.

Many ask me how I could forgive Sam for what he did to me, and my response is: Nothing Sam did to me, no matter how wrong, could ever be worth it to me to disappoint God! God asked us to forgive our enemies so we may be forgiven. By forgiving Sam I have allowed myself to live free of bitterness and resentment. I refuse to allow him to have any hold on me. The act of forgiving is when you are able to lift someone up to the Lord and pray that He have mercy on their soul. I did just that, and I can say that I am truly free of him and feel liberated, and I am so much at peace with everything that took place.

Ironically, the day Sam tried to murder me was the best day of my life. I am blessed beyond what mere words can express. Since this incident, the Lord has become my best friend, my comforter, my counselor, my soul mate, and indeed my everything! He took me through wrenching human perils and through death, to show me that He is all I need. He was always there, but He revealed Himself that day, as He carried me gently through suffering, by His love and tenderness.

Furthermore, I have also forgiven Paul. Even though his goal in life was to destroy me, I never spoke ill about him in front of our son and daughter. I understood how important it was for them to grow up maintaining their respect and love for their father. The children were hurt enough being caught between us and the court system; I did not want to add to their pain. As the years passed, Paul became a better father to them and I continued to nourish their relationship with him. I eventually became friends with his new wife who was a very good stepmother to both of them. I have always been truly grateful for her presence in their lives.

It was only a few years ago that Paul told Colleen to ask me to forgive him. Colleen told him that I had forgiven him a long time ago. His response was that he knew that I forgave him, but he wanted me to know that he was sorry for all the pain he caused me. We finally have peace between us.

My Sweet Encounter with Life

"And if you faithfully obey the voice of the
LORD your God.... all these blessings shall
come upon you and overtake you..."
—Deuteronomy 28:1a-2a (ESV)

It was a sunny afternoon in Southern California when I stepped out of my condominium heading to the elevator, and there stood my neighbor. He was tall and handsome with silver locks of hair and a silver mustache. He looked towards me with his piercing blue eyes and greeted me with a warm smile. I had heard that a widower had bought the unit next to me a few months before. Assuming he was the new neighbour, I intentionally avoided him because I did not want to give the wrong impression, that I was some desperate, single woman living next door.

By this time, it had been about ten years since my encounter with death and I had lived alone working as a Chief Financial Officer/Chief Operations Officer. I also spent some time traveling throughout the US, East Africa and South Africa, reaching thousands of people by speaking about my encounter with death. My daughter Colleen was living in San Francisco, studying law at Berkeley. My son Andrew had gotten married and had moved to Maryland after earning his MBA. I lived alone but was never lonely. I was happy and satisfied with my intimate relationship with God and never even considered meeting another man. I did not date for ten years, so when a widower moved in next door, I did not want to give him the wrong impression—I was content being alone.

Robert and I chatted at the elevator, and we agreed that we should get together over coffee and learn more about each other. We agreed on meeting a couple of days later at his flat. It was lovely getting to know him. He was kind and thoughtful. He was a retired Navy Captain of two nuclear submarines, who lost his wife to cancer almost a year before. We had a great time talking and chit-chatting, but one statement he made, right before I left, touched my heart; He said that he was lonely. The loss of his precious wife had taken a toll on him and left him longing for companionship once again. I invited him for dinner a few days later, and we discovered that we had many things in common—we both really enjoyed going to the movies, which made for our next date.

As the days passed, I realized that God put Robert in my life. I had forgotten there were still good men that existed, and he was one of them. I never thought I would consider another relationship with a man. I never searched or wished for a man, nor did I long for one. I was convinced that it would be unfair for a man to fall in love with me. I felt that God fully occupied my mind, heart, and soul. I would not be able to share myself with anyone else. I also did not want any distractions from my service to the Lord and my mission of being His ambassador. I felt no man would understand my intimate relationship with my God and may even get jealous. But to my surprise, my heart opened up for Robert, and I fell in love with him, and realized that my heart could handle the love of a man along with the greater love of my God.

All I was truly seeking was God, but somehow God blessed me with more. He blessed me with an extremely kind, thoughtful, and gentle soul. He blessed me with Robert. *But seek first the kingdom of God and his righteousness, and all these things will be added to you* (Mathew 6:33, ESV).

Reflections

I am the LORD your God, who brought you out
of the land of Egypt, out of the house of slavery.
"You shall have no other gods before me.
—Exodus 20:2–3 (ESV)

I asked the Lord why Sam got away with what he did. The Lord responded, "Child, this was not about Sam. It was about you! I had to free you from your bondage." I had been in bondage and had not even realized it. I had been addicted to a man. Most of us think an addiction is related to alcohol or drugs, but many people are hooked to a toxic partner and don't even know it, nor do they realize how harmful this condition is.

My biggest problem was that I could never imagine my life without Sam. He was "my everything." I remarried him because I was afraid to grow old alone, even though there were warning signs, during the time in Dubai, that I could not trust him. Finally, the Lord had to shut my eyes, so I could see what this man was capable of doing.

As I look back and see how Sam got away with my attempted murder, I am somehow relieved. If he had been convicted, he would have served an average jail time, roughly between five and fifteen years, with a chance of early release due to good behavior. Once he had done his time, he would be out and most likely be seeking revenge to harm me and my loved ones, for the rest of our lives. My life would have been negatively altered if I had to live watching my back, and in fear for my loved ones. Therefore, I am relieved knowing that he is far away.

Grief Examined

In looking back, I have wondered why I was vulnerable to a narcissist like Paul and fell prey to a sociopath like Sam. Perhaps it was because I was easygoing, trusting, and kind-hearted. Perhaps it was because I had felt so secure and taken care of by my father, that I assumed all men were as kind and trustworthy as he was.

My sister Nadia, a genuinely attractive woman, experienced some of the same things that I had, such as going through a failed marriage. How she loved our father who was so strong and reassuring! She was very close to him, so of course his sudden tragic death devastated her and her life was never the same.

Words of Warning!

How many young women rush into marriage, as I did with Paul, wanting stability and security, or put a man on the throne of their hearts where God belongs, as I did with Sam? I would like to advise them to seek the Lord with all their hearts to reveal the right companion for them. Many skip this part: when you seek the Lord, make sure you wait and hear what He reveals. Most of the time, we request the Lord to bless our choice of companion without waiting to hear if He even approves of our choice.

Marrying a godly man is a wise choice. A man who truly fears and loves the Lord, will love his wife. When a woman is treated with real love, she will naturally respect her husband and cherish him. This is God's plan for marriage. Going to church and practicing rituals does not make a man or a woman godly, just as my sister Mira always said, "Standing in a garage does not make you a car." Rather, godliness arises from a pure relationship with the Lord. When you make the Lord the central part of your marriage and lean on His everlasting arms, all the rest of God's provisions make sense. Without Him, even the best that life offers becomes a trial.

I often wonder how many people get away with poisoning their loved ones, drowning them in a bathtub, and then claiming they overdosed, drowned or committed suicide. It is so sad to know that even today in the United States, women are still not taken seriously when it comes to domestic abuse. Even if a woman is competent and credible, no matter what status a woman holds, she is not taken seriously when it comes to accusations of abuse. I hope my story will inspire some legislation that will make it mandatory for hospitals to conduct routine heavy-metal testing on patients, in case of potential foul play.

Who Is Ana?

I am nobody. My frailties are many. I have exposed my faults, small, and looming, and my Lord knows them all. Yet He spared me from death, saved me from paralysis, and best of all showed me the joy of trusting in Him. I never believed I would fellowship with the Lord of my faith in this lifetime. Who is Ana that He would consider me? The better question is, "Who is He that He considers the downtrodden, weak, and powerless?" He is a God greater than our ability to comprehend, but He lowers Himself to our level to encourage, nurture, and deliver us from every affliction. I no longer fear death, as I know God is there to prepare me, coach me, and accompany me into Heaven. Death is not an end, but rather a sweet journey into a new, overwhelming beginning. When we die, there is neither darkness nor silence. Our soul just keeps on going after leaving our body behind.

Near Death Experiences

John Burke, author and founding pastor of Gateway Church in Austin, Texas, has studied near-death experiences (NDEs) for over thirty-five years. Here is his explanation of why NDEs are important and help promote faith, including his own:

> "Heaven and near-death experiences (NDEs) – of people who clinically died, were resuscitated, and claimed to have gotten a peek into the afterlife – have been a hot topic of late. I've never been one to gullibly believe every story of seeing Heaven. Yet over the past thirty-five years, I've studied or heard close to 1,000 near-death stories (the Gallup Poll found 1 in 25 people have had an NDE—so there are millions). Through my study, I saw amazing commonalities – intriguing, detailed descriptions by doctors, professors, commercial airline pilots, children, people from around the globe. Each gave a slightly different angle to what started to look like a very similar picture.
>
> During that same thirty-five-year time frame, I went from a career in engineering to full-time

ministry. I'm now a convinced Christian, but I was not always convinced. As a former skeptic, my passion is helping skeptical people consider the many reasons that keep me believing.

Some Christians say that NDEs should be rejected because these tales of the afterlife deny the sufficiency of Scripture and therefore add to God's revelation. I respectfully disagree. I have found that the common NDE experiences actually are aligned with Scripture. Near-death experiences add vivid color and texture to Scripture's picture of Heaven."

More than 900 articles on NDEs have been published in scholarly literature like the *Journal of the American Medical Association* and *Psychiatry*.[3]

Why the Holy Spirit?

Most people who have NDEs share the encounter of a great light and an overwhelming love and compassion by a great being of power. Some refer to Him as the Creator of the Universe while others say they encountered their own God. Some encounter Jesus, and others encounter a being of Light.

---

[3] John Burke, "Imagine Heaven," last accessed August 8, 2021, at https://sidroth.org/newsletter/january-2019-newsletter/#.

So why am I one of the rare people who encountered the Being who revealed Himself as the Holy Spirit? The answer was finally revealed to me: I encountered the Holy Spirit **while** I was dying, **not after** I died. He was only on this side, on earth, comforting me while I endured the poisoning, rape, paralysis, and suffocation. When I died and crossed over to the other side, I saw Jesus in Heaven and not the Holy Spirit. This is confusing to some Christians because our core faith is based on the Trinity being One, but I also encountered each as a separate being as well. I am sure it is especially hard to really wrap one's head around it.

In simple terms, the Holy Spirit was the Spirit of death. Actually, He was the Spirit of Light, because there was no darkness or silence when I died; my soul just kept on going to the other side, the afterlife. Most people who have experienced an NDE have told their stories of what took place after they were dead and what they encountered after they crossed over. My encounter was not only what took place when I crossed over, but also what occurred right before that, when I was hovering between life and death, and how He comforted me while I was dying and up to my last breath of air.

Leaning on Our Ever-Present Helper

The message that has been put on my heart is to help everyone realize that we have a Comforter and Counselor who is with us 24/7. He does not come and go. He is always there for us and will never leave us, just as Jesus promised: *And I will ask the Father, and he will give you another Helper, to be with you forever* (John 14:16, ESV).

Many people feel that they should only call on the Lord when they are in deep trouble or have something serious to worry about. They don't realize that they have a friend whom they can count on with every decision, no matter how small it is. Furthermore, many Christians can only relate to Jesus and miss out on the wonderful constant presence of the Holy Spirit who was sent to us by Jesus to take His place on earth:

> *Nevertheless, I tell you the truth: it is to*
> *your advantage that I go away, for if I do*
> *not go away, the Helper will not come to*
> *you. But if I go, I will send him to you.*
> —John 16:7, ESV

The Comforter is in every little detail of our lives. He is our advisor and advocate, the One who has our backs constantly. Growing up, I used to often pray that the Lord would give me the gift of wisdom, that I would wake up one day and find myself wise. I finally realized that the Holy Spirit is wisdom waiting to be utilized by us.

I truly am convinced that the Holy Spirit is the kingdom of heaven on Earth. Jesus said not to believe when someone tells you the kingdom of heaven is over there or over here, but it is within, which proves that He is referring to the Holy Spirit. Jesus said, *"Nor will people say, Look! Here! or, See there! For behold, the kingdom of God is within you and among you"* (Luke 17:21 AMPC).

Discovering and acknowledging the "Spirit of God" is like finding the most awesome jewel in the world. He is better than diamonds and gold:

> *"The kingdom of heaven is like treasure*
> *hidden in a field, which a man found and*
> *covered up. Then in his joy he goes and*
> *sells all that he has and buys that field.*
> —Matthew 13:44, ESV

He is the most precious gift the Lord has ever given to us, and most of the time we don't even acknowledge Him.

The Holy Spirit will never impose His presence on us, neither does He leave us if we don't acknowledge Him. He is exceedingly patient, and He awaits us. I have a new understanding that this is why He has so much time to count every hair on our head as the Scriptures states. *Why, even the hairs of your head are all numbered. Fear not; you are of more value than many sparrows* (Luke 12:7, ESV). However, we are richly rewarded when we acknowledge His presence—the more we acknowledge Him, the more active He will be in our lives.

We have a choice. We can try to make it on our own and struggle, or we can choose to make life a little easier by utilizing God's Counselor who knows our future and knows what is good for us: *For I know the plans I have for you, declares the LORD, plans for welfare and not for evil, to give you a future and a hope* (Jeremiah 29:11, ESV). This is exactly like a parent who advises his or her child on an issue. The parent knows the consequences of the wrong decision their child will make, but the child, especially a teenager, feels that he or she knows it all and does not need to listen. The same is true of our Father in Heaven. He wants to spare us pain and suffering if only we would listen to His gentle whispers that are spoken by His sweet Spirit who He gifted us!

"If you then, who are evil, know how to
give good gifts to your children, how much
more will the heavenly Father give the
Holy Spirit to those who ask him!"
—Luke 11:13 ESV

Just as He is with us in life, the Lord escorts us through the amazing transition we call death to what He has prepared for us. Experiencing this has transformed me. I used to love God but now I am in love with God.

There is no need for us to place romantic love or any person— man, woman, or child—on the throne of our hearts. The place for our worship is meant for God alone, and any other person or thing placed in that position of supreme honor will fail us. God is my strength and my refuge. If He would come to me and bring comfort, He will do so for others who love and trust Him. I do not believe that we must be at the brink of death to invite Him into our lives. The many sorrows that come upon us are many doors through which we feel our need for Him, but He is ever present and ready to help us. I have found the hidden treasure that the Bible says is worth selling everything else to obtain. God's presence in our lives is valuable and worth finding. I want to shout from the highest mountain: "He is in every little detail of our lives!" The sweet companionship of the Holy Spirit is more than we could hope for in this lifetime. So, go ahead and acknowledge Him—start enjoying a piece of Heaven on Earth today!

Printed in the United States
by Baker & Taylor Publisher Services